# CLASSIC
# QUEEN

## PHOTOGRAPHS AND TEXT BY MICK ROCK

**OMNIBUS PRESS**

This edition published 2016 by Omnibus Press
(A Division of Music Sales Limited)

ISBN: 978.1.78558.228.8
Order No: OP56859

Exclusive Distributors
Music Sales Limited,
14/15 Berners Street,
London, W1T 3LJ

Visit Omnibus Press on the web at www.omnibuspress.com

Created and produced by Palazzo Editions Ltd
2 Wood Street, Bath, BA1 2JQ, United Kingdom
www.palazzoeditions.com

Designed by Adrian Cross

10 9 8 7 6 5 4 3 2 1

Printed and bound in China

A catalogue record for this book is available from the British Library.

# CONTENTS

Following page *QUEEN II* SHOOT 1973

## "BRITAIN'S BIGGEST UNKNOWNS"

– that was the headline which UK music paper *Sounds* used to usher in 1974. Queen took third place in that issue's Best New British Band poll – behind Nazareth and that decade's Blue – and by the end of the year had had the kind of success that would have justified the top spot. But it wasn't beginner's luck. Queen weren't an overnight sensation. Their lives weren't changed by winning *New Faces* or *Opportunity Knocks*, the *X Factor* of their day. They had been putting in the groundwork for years. They had invested time, effort and sweat into building their dreams. And in 1973 it began to pay off. But it could have been so different.

The early 1970s were a time of experimentation and excess. Glitter and glam. Androgyny was the rage, mono-sexuality the cage. Gloss was the word on everybody's lips; mascara the word on everybody's eyes. As David Bowie recalls, the most pressing question of any given day was "Greasepaint or pancake?"

Confusion abounded. Bowie was the "phallus in pigtails." Long hair and bare chests teased photographers. And music just got that little bit more interesting.

Lou Reed hadn't played on his own first album. His do-wop street Dylan act fell on busy ears. Bowie rode to the rescue and produced *Transformer*. We all took a walk on the wild side. Reed was introduced to eyeliner and New York's deity of doom was born. Angela Bowie remembers him "wearing heavy mascara and jet black lipstick with matching nail polish, plus a tight little Errol Flynn-as Robin Hood body shirt." "The Phantom of Rock" was the moniker Reed's label gave their urban poet. He was a man literally transformed. And Mick Rock took the cover picture. "People think that's studio work but it's not," he recalls. "It was a live shot. The energy comes from the fact he's looking away."

Mick Rock knows a thing or two. Mick was the man who shot the 70s. Mick took the pictures Iggy Pop now uses for memories. He conceived the reinvention of Lou Reed. He was Ziggy Stardust's personal photographer and diarist. And in 1974 he created, with the help of Marlene Dietrich, the defining image of Queen. You know the one. It's as synonymous with Freddie and Co three decades later as it was then. It's been in videos, in magazines and even in movies.

But more of that later.

Bowie was big news in 1972 and 1973. But he wasn't the first of the Colorful Ones. That was Mark Feld. Marc Bolan to you and me. He took his name from an abbreviation of his hero Bob Dylan. Or was it the fact he shared a flat with the Likely Lad James Bolam? It matters not. It's the effect we remember. It's what the name stands for, not what it means. "David Jones" was taken. He was a Monkee. "Bowie" is a type of knife, as is "Jagger." *Stardust* was a David Essex film – but only after Ziggy had died.

And Mercury is a god. He ruled the land of Rhye, a world of ogres and fairy kings created by Farook Bulsara.

But more of that later.

Bolan's glitter-splashed T.Rex put a foot in the black-and-white media door. But it was David Bowie who kicked it down. "Bolan was Glam 1.0," he says. "We were straining in the wings with versions 1.01 and 1.02, while Marc was still struggling with satin."

Then there was Gary Glitter, Sweet, Slade, Roxy Music, Mott the Hoople – and Larry Lurex. Lurex was a "tribute" featuring Freddie Mercury, Brian May and Roger Taylor. It annoyed the Glitter fan club but it did not chart. Which is just as well. That is not how Queen should begin.

America succumbed to the color of the 70s with the next wave. On the East Coast the New York Dolls introduced dirty leather glam. Vince Furnier added eyeliner and executions to Alice Cooper and Suzi Quatro canned the can in Devil Gate Drive. Detroit and New York vied with each other for bragging rights, for dominion over this thing called glam. But the real story, the real second chapter, was happening in London. Via the West Country, Leicester, Middlesex – and Zanzibar.

Lou Reed mainlined the Beat of Kerouac and Ginsberg. Bowie tripped the names of Burroughs, Brecht and Baudelaire.

Queen didn't read. They rocked.

John Lennon. Buddy Holly. Elvis Presley. Led Zeppelin. The Who.

And Jimi Hendrix. On 18 September 1970 Freddie Mercury and Roger Taylor closed their Kensington Market clothes stall in deference to Hendrix's sad passing. Mercury cried for hours. At rehearsal that evening he performed "Voodoo Chile."

Freddie never met Hendrix. But Brian did. His university band, 1984, supported the guitarist at an Imperial College gig. It was 13 May 1967 – and Hendrix was late leaving his dressing room. "Which way's the stage, man?"

Queen were a band of contradictions. Peerless imaginations and musical gifts, constructed on solid foundations. Bowie built elaborate characters who came alive on stage; John Deacon built amplifiers so the band could be heard. Iggy Pop experimented with every ingestible drug; Brian May experimented with his own homemade guitar created from a fireplace, bike parts and buttons.

Bowie studied mime under Lindsay Kemp; May was invited to work at Jodrell Bank under Professor Sir Bernard Lovell. David later played Warhol on film; Brian presented *The Sky at Night*.

They did things differently.

Queen were always more than the sum of their parts.

A postcard pinned to the Imperial College noticeboard asking for a "Ginger Baker/Mitch Mitchell type drummer" caught the eye of ex-Cousin Jacks and Reaction member Roger Taylor's attention. Brian May and fellow 1984 stalwart Tim Staffell were impressed with his audition and the three-piece Smile was born.

They were nearly there. "Earth," "Polar Bear," and "Step on Me" from Smile's mini-LP could have been Queen songs; "Doin' All Right," co-written by Brian and Tim, actually became one when it appeared on Queen's debut album, sung by Freddie in his best Staffell impression. Smile's first gig was in support of Pink Floyd on 26 October 1968. Then came spots under T.Rex and Yes and one appearance above Paul Rodgers' Free. The pieces were almost in place.

Freddie Bulsara studied art with Staffell at Ealing College. At first he tagged along to shows because Staffell was a friend. But then he became hooked. Freddie knew he wanted to perform.

For a while Freddie and his immaculate satin pants were part of Liverpudlian band Ibex. Back in London he then fronted Sour Milk Sea and later Wreckage. But the band he really wanted to be in was Smile.

In March 1970 he got his chance. Staffell left to join Humpy Bong and Freddie quit Wreckage.

The new trio needed a new name. Old friends, Brian and Roger, relative veterans of the music business, both agreed on "Grand Dance" – a phrase from the C.S. Lewis trilogy *Out of the Silent Planet*. It was two against one. It should have been a done deal. But Freddie never was any good at math. He had a vision. In April 1970 that vision – Queen – came to life.

The jigsaw still needed one more piece. Freddie only replaced Staffell's vocals and his role as logo designer. The band required a bass player.

Former Reaction bandmate of Roger's, Mike Grose, was chosen to be the fourth man at Queen's first ever gig on 27 June 1970. The band opened the set with a reworked Wreckage song called "Stone Cold Crazy" – which would appear on their *Sheer Heart Attack* album four years later, credited to Queen. By August Grose decided he needed to get a "proper" job. "I thought, even then, that this band might one day make it big," he recalls. "But that didn't stop me wanting to get out."

Bass player number two, Barry Mitchell, lasted four months and several prestigious gigs – including one at The Cavern in Liverpool – before he too tired of the lack of serious income. Ever the students, Roger, Freddie and Brian seemed content to hone their stagecraft and write songs, convinced that success would come eventually; Mitchell needed more than their slight return.

His replacement, "Doug," lasted just two gigs before he was fired. Doug's crime? Attempting to steal the limelight from Freddie. That would never do. Queen didn't have room for that kind of bass player. "We needed someone quiet who would fit in with us without too much trouble," Roger specifies.

They needed John Deacon.

That should have been it. The fairy story dictates that they all lived happily ever after surrounded by gold discs and platinum blondes. It was February 1971. Bowie was writing *Hunky Dory*, the Rolling Stones were about to release *Sticky Fingers*. "Hot Love," "Get It On," and "Jeepster" were pouring out of Bolan. The time was right.

But Queen didn't have a deal. They had a stage act, they had songs, they had costumes designed by Freddie and friends. But they didn't have a deal.

So they became guinea pigs. De Lane Lea studios in Wembley needed musicians to try out their new state of the art equipment. In exchange the band could use the studio during down time to record their own music. It wasn't an appearance on *Top of the Pops* but Queen felt it was a step in the right direction.

Progress was slow. Painfully slow. Over the course of a year, they recorded five self-penned songs: "Keep Yourself Alive," "Great King Rat," "The Night Comes Down," "Jesus" and "Liar." The latter, released two years later as a single in America, began life as "Lover" when Freddie wrote it with Mike Bersin for Ibex. It was radically reworked by Queen for their debut album but credit went to Mercury. "As far as I'm concerned, the person who wrote the words has effectively written the song," he said.

Fortunes changed when producers John Anthony and Roy Thomas Baker came to scout De Lane Lea for possible future use. They were both impressed by the young band and reported back to their contacts at a management company called Trident who several months later signed them on a "catch all" golden handcuffs contract.

But still no fairytale ending.

The Trident deal again only let them record when the studios weren't booked. Queen were the same age as acts like Elton John and David Bowie. They should have been musical contemporaries, not office juniors. How galling having to wait for the crumbs to drop from their fellow artists' recording tables. "We were into glam rock before groups like The Sweet and Bowie and we were worried because we might have come too late," Brian admits.

In 1973 it happened. Their debut album was released. Brian helped design the sleeve. Their producer wanted to call it *Deary Me*. It was three years in the making and it got good reviews.

But nobody bought it.

What did it matter that Eric Clapton would later call Brian the best guitarist in the world if no one else heard him? How did it help that Freddie Mercury was hailed as the most energetic stage performer since Mick Jagger if audiences didn't know his name? What was the point of being glam if no one could see you glitter? Queen had the looks, the dynamic front man, the pretty boy drummer, the songs, the question-marked sexuality, the drive, the intelligence and above all the talent.

But they didn't have an audience.

They needed help. They needed exposure. They needed an image. They needed fans to know they were out there. That they were part of The Scene.

The first step was to leave the design of their next album to the professionals.

There was only one choice. Get the man who took the Phallic Guitar picture of Bowie. Get the guy who did the covers of *Transformer* and *Raw Power*. Get Mick Rock.

But could he help? Could he do for them what he'd done for so many others? It was a big ask. Queen had seen off three bass players. They had no hits, no money. No real hope for the second album, the one they wanted to call *Over the Top*.

They had no mass of fans. No unmistakable public image. No fairytale ending.

And then Mick Rock showed them a picture of Marlene Dietrich...

# CLASSIC QUEEN BY MICK ROCK

I was born on the Holland Road at the corner of Elsham Road, London, a couple of streets up from the Shepherd's Bush roundabout; within fifteen doors of where Freddie Mercury and Mary Austin used to live on Holland Road when I first knew them.

When I was eighteen years old I went to study modern languages at Caius College, Cambridge. I was involved with a group of student hippies and through them met Syd Barrett at a Christmas party during my first year. It was 1966, before Pink Floyd had made their first record. *Piper at the Gates of Dawn* came out in 1967. Later I used to go and see Pink Floyd down at the U.F.O. Club, along with The Soft Machine and The Crazy World of Arthur Brown.

I'd always had it in mind to be a writer. My late school and college heroes were the wild and aberrant bohemian Symbolist poets of late nineteenth-century Paris, such as Baudelaire, Rimbaud, Nerval, Gautier, Verlaine and their absinthe- and hashish-stimulated cohorts (and their infamous "Club des Hashishiens"). But almost by accident I wandered into photography. In the beginning it was, in truth, all about the other sex (Ah! *Quelle surprise!*). I was hanging out in the college room of a friend with a particularly pretty young blonde lady, and in a playful effort to impress (as I recall, our senses were, shall we say, somewhat impaired by sensory over- indulgence), I grabbed at my friend's 35mm camera. I had very little idea of what I was up to; my only previous experience had been with the family Kodak Brownie on summer holidays. I started jumping around, pointing the camera at my lady friend – who clearly found my antics very amusing – and it seemed that every time I touched the camera, it went off... Very sexual, no doubt. Later, when I asked my friend to open up the camera, we found there was no film in it!!

Of course, all I'd have shot would have been some girl sitting in a room looking a bit wide-eyed! But somehow the camera fuelled my perceptions. It was as if the universe was on fire! There was a lot of roaring, rushing and major sensory amplification. That experience embedded itself in my psyche and became associated with the camera. It inspired me to want to do it again. The next time there was film in the camera, and I took some photographs of another lady friend, which I still have. Perhaps the camera gave me another weapon in my armory. Anyway, most of those early pictures were pictures of girlfriends or friends or my mates' girlfriends.

I left Cambridge with my degree and an interest in Rimbaud. I thought how great it would be to live the life of a bohemian poet. But I got my most positive reactions to the results of my photographic endeavours. "It was *Blow Up*, Mick, wasn't it?" A lot of photographers say that they were inspired by *Blow Up*, because that was the first film whose central character was a photographer. In fact, the character was loosely based on David Bailey. But I didn't have any raging ambition to be a photographer, certainly not a fashion photographer. But I was interested in movies, so I got a grant to study film for a year.

At film school I naturally watched a lot of films, and even made a couple of short experimental ones. I kept taking pictures because I could do that without any help from anyone. I became increasingly entranced with the instant access to imagery a camera gave. I knew a few musicians and they started to ask me to take photos for them. Syd was my first key session, but I also photographed The Pretty Things, the Ainsley Dunbar Retaliation, and group called Eire Apparent who were managed by

"I remember
Freddie telling me,
'The most important
thing is to live
a fabulous life.

As long as
it's fabulous,
I don't care
how long it is.'

Freddie Mercury was one
of my favourite
human beings,
a gem of a man."

*MR {1995}*

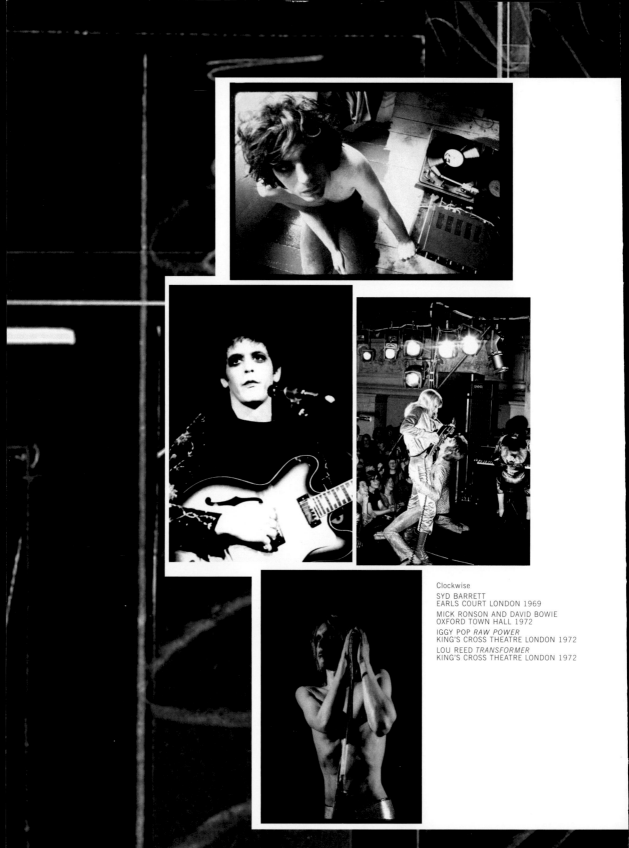

Clockwise
SYD BARRETT
EARLS COURT LONDON 1969
MICK RONSON AND DAVID BOWIE
OXFORD TOWN HALL 1972
IGGY POP *RAW POWER*
KING'S CROSS THEATRE LONDON 1972
LOU REED *TRANSFORMER*
KING'S CROSS THEATRE LONDON 1972

Chas Chandler and had just come back from a tour of America with Hendrix. And they paid me!! Whoopee. It would be maybe £20 or £25 and I suddenly realized you could make money from this. That was terrific: much better than getting a "real" job!!

After film school I worked briefly with with an album cover design company called Hipgnosis. I worked with them on a few album covers, such as Rory Gallagher's first solo LP. And I remember shooting the centerfold for *Meddle*, the Pink Floyd album, on 5x4 plate camera. You can see from my pictures that my work was different from the Hipgnosis look. I loved their work but realized they weren't really about the personalities: they were mostly about the design and the production. They dealt with a lot of musicians but they rarely photographed them; their album covers were mostly concepts that didn't involve shooting the musicians themselves. But it was the musicians that turned me on. I liked the things that happened in the chemistry of the moment. I liked to work in an improvisational way. I liked the way great things happened in the interplay between myself and my subject. The Hipgnosis approach produced great results, but it wasn't how I liked to work. We were working in the same field, but I had a different muse!! So I left after a few months to pursue my own visual odyssey.

Although the first monies I made were strictly with my camera, I soon realized that my Cambridge education had lent me a way with words and that I could augment my income if I wrote articles and illustrated them with photos. So I would do both. I wrote the last ever interview with Syd Barrett for *Rolling Stone* magazine. Later I also did features on Rory Gallagher, David Bowie, Iggy Pop, Freddie Mercury, Lou Reed, and so on, for a variety of publications including *19* magazine, *Club International*, *Rock Scene*, *Honey*, in fact for whoever I could talk into commissioning me!! Some of my very earliest pictures of Bowie were for *Club International*. In those days the lot of most photographers was much more modest than it is today.

It all started to change for me in the spring and summer of 1972 as David Bowie rose to fame. Bowie was still relatively obscure when I first interviewed and shot him; in early March of 1972, Ziggy was just at the starting gates. I also shot Lou Reed and Iggy Pop's first ever shows in Europe which produced both the *Transformer* and *Raw Power* album covers. Lou was still an underground "cult" figure, whose Velvet Underground and first solo albums had been complete commercial failures. The same was true of the first two Iggy and the Stooges albums. The moment it all changed gear for me was the publication in *Melody Maker* in June of 1972 of the infamous "guitar fellatio" photo of Bowie and Mick Ronson at Oxford Town Hall. This was that shot that put my name on the map. Suddenly I was in demand, and my camera was clearly speaking louder than my words... In that early Bowie period I became a fully-fledged rock 'n' roll propagandist. I took pictures, put together special setups, did album covers and some projection work on David's stage show, wrote for magazines, and shot "promo films" ("John I'm Only Dancing," "Jean Genie," "Space Oddity," and "Life On Mars"). Truly, 1972 was a banner year for me. I worked with Bowie, Iggy, Lou Reed. I also art-directed and designed the album package for Mott the Hoople's Bowie-produced "All The Young Dudes." "Glam" revved into high gear, and I was the photographer in demand. In Bowie's wake came Roxy Music, Cockney Rebel and of course Queen. The glitter scene that Marc Bolan and T.Rex had spearheaded was now dismissed as being lightweight and purely for teens. This new variation was much more sophisticated and a lot more decadent in tone and creativity.

In 1973, Queen was managed by Trident Audio Productions who owned Trident Studios, where *Ziggy Stardust*, *All The Young Dudes*, and *Transformer* had been recorded. Trident acted as a production company, but they also managed certain acts, and had the connections to strike deals with the record labels. Ken Scott was part of Trident Audio Productions and he was the one who mentioned Queen to me. Ken was co-producer and engineer on David Bowie's *Hunky Dory*, *Ziggy Stardust* and *Pin Ups*.

One day during the recording of *Pin Ups* at Chateau d'Hérouville near Paris, Ken said to me, "Mick there's this band, Queen. They love your work, especially the things you've done with David and Lou, and they really want you to shoot them. They're very serious, and when we get back to town I want to turn you on to them." They were completely unknown; nobody I knew had ever heard of them. When their first album, *Queen* had been released, it had gone virtually unnoticed. But I was curious. Ken's enthusiasm for the group had whetted my appetite. So I called him and he set the meeting up. It was September of 1973 when I met with Queen in the conference room in Trident Studios.

# "...so they just said,

## 'Come on in, we like you, we want you to do this for us, and this is who we are, and this is the music...'

# Well, the music..."

*MR*

"When we started off,
rock bands were all
wearing jeans

— and suddenly
here's Freddie Mercury
in a Zandra Rhodes frock
with make-up
and black
nail varnish.

It was outrageous!"

*Freddie Mercury {1971}*

IMPERIAL COLLEGE GIG NOVEMBER 1973

Of course, Queen told me right up front that they were destined for success, that bright afternoon in the autumn of 1973 when we first met. They sought me out because they wanted to graft some of that decadent "glam" sensibility onto their own image.

We were all of similar ages, plus I had a little bit of a track record by then. And for them that was significant. But they certainly weren't sitting there waiting nervously for me. It was immediately clear I wouldn't have to coax a "star" attitude out of them. They were there already, in their minds at least. Yet I still hadn't a clue how they sounded. After pumping me with enthusiasm, they played me the *Queen II* acetate, and I recognized at once the source of their confidence. This *was* something special. It was a fast and very potent seduction. I was primed for some serious rock 'n' roll collusion. If you listen to *Queen II* now it's not as sophisticated as they became a little later but it is still a remarkable album.

They were looking for two things. They wanted some pictures to help publicize the first album, which had already been released. At this point they had nothing going other than enormous talent. It hadn't yet translated into commercial recognition. They hoped that I could conjure up some images that would attract some attention. They also needed an album cover for *Queen II*. The main thing I took away from that initial rendezvous was their palpable confidence…

I was very comfortable with them from the giddy up – and giddy our sessions often were. A democratic combo, they all needed to be consulted on the process of our image-building enterprise. Always bubbling away, overwhelming you with charm and determination, they were in a hurry: they wanted the world and they wanted it no later than teatime on Friday.

Although very inexperienced in the ways of the camera – our first session was the first time they set foot in a photo studio – they were obviously well versed in the ancient and delectable art of preening. They came prepared and were totally self-styled in their dress. And they loved the mirror. They didn't strike me as unduly narcissistic however; they were simply concerned that they looked right. They had weighed well the importance of the visual sell. Their American manager, Jack Nelson had been hired by Trident, and his brief passage with Queen was pretty rough from my observations. They questioned him about everything. They were very much concerned about quality control in all aspects of their career, even though they were learning on the job… I remember once being in the office and a photograph had been published by *Creem* magazine, which they had not approved, and poor Jack got hell for it. They were hardly known but they understood the importance of controlling their image from the start

In the early days I had been a bit wide-eyed about rock 'n' roll, but by the time Queen came along I'd been around the block a little and I was more sophisticated in certain ways about dealing with situations and figuring out whose opinion carried the most weight. Freddie and Roger were the two prime salesmen, and certainly they were the most extroverted. Brian had opinions, but he was gentler in his expression of them. He was just naturally friendly, whereas Freddie and Roger were active *charmers*. Their attitude was more like, "If you want to work with us, you've got to believe in us." They were impressed with me because of who I had worked with, but they wanted to let me know that they weren't too impressed…!

So I had to love their music too, to get the gig, which wasn't difficult since the acetate they had played me was so powerful and impressive. And I told them so – and sealed the deal!

Improbable as it might seem for a band that was so painstaking over its image, Queen and before them Roger and Brian's band Smile, had paid their rock 'n' roll dues and done the battered old van thing, crisscrossing the nation in varying degrees of discomfort. Fortified only by the unique way in which youth somehow makes it all seem like fun, they certainly weren't in it for the money because they were barely breaking even.

I found Queen to be very much who they were from the get-go. They weren't pretending to be in the working-clas tradition of British bands. Of course there were a number of acts (especially the northern-spawned ones) who genuinely were working class, but many of the Home Counties acts really weren't, although they were all good at faking a cockney accent. Pete Townshend and Mick Jagger were most decidedly well brought up middle class lads, for all the rebellion in their attitude and accent. But Queen were of a new breed and they didn't try to hide it. They were all middle class and well educated. Roger was training to be a dentist, John and Brian were working on PhDs and Freddie had been to art school, the breeding ground for many of the great early British rockers such as John Lennon, Keith Richards, Pete Townshend, Syd Barrett and David Bowie etc.

Queen had come together as a foursome in 1971, following the demise of Smile. Brian and Roger had recruited Freddie as their new singer and then found a bass player in John. At the time the four were all still preoccupied with various day-jobs. Although ostensibly students, Freddie and Roger were running a clothes stall in Kensington market, selling their own designs as their academic careers went on the back burner. They weren't doing much in the way of business but it was here that Queen's unique style had its beginning.

Brian and John were altogether more serious about their studies, both up to their ears in the sciences with Brian doing a degree in astrophysics. It wasn't until Queen were signed up to EMI in 1972 that they actually completely let go and turned professional; as ever, Queen didn't leave much to chance. Their debut album *Queen* initially didn't do much in the UK, though it sold reasonably well in the States without them ever having been there. But despite the initial indifference, their homeland was waking up to the fact that this band, this extraordinary looking foursome, was indeed something special.

# "...this was something special...it was a fast and very potent seduction...I was primed for some serious rock 'n' roll collusion..." MR

*"...I don't recall Queen ever getting hung up on setbacks. They would move on very fast psychologically. They wanted success badly; nothing was going to bring them down. They'd talk about the positive things, they weren't floored by anything..." MR*

"It's surprising really that we had so much confidence even in those days, when absolutely nothing was happening. I suppose we always had a good time…Believe it or not, we are not in a hurry. We'd rather it all took much longer. It's important that we keep control. It must all go the right way otherwise we're wasting our own and everyone else's time. We know we're good, we know what we want, and it's no good anyone trying to talk us out of it."
   *Freddie Mercury {1974}*

"The music press
have been pretty unfair to us.
We are basically a rock
band. I think we're good
writers, and we want
to play good music, no matter
how much of a slagging
we get. The music is the
most important factor."

*Freddie Mercury {1974}*

The very first time I saw the band play was at their watershed gig at Imperial College, London on 18th November 1973. It was also the first time I saw them through my camera lens. I don't recall them getting a boisterous welcome. But certainly they had some kind of buzz going for them and there was a real sense of curiosity in the hall. This was the first time an audience had turned up in significant numbers specifically to see Queen and they were enthralled by the high drama of a band that was clearly destined for bigger things.

Before that night Queen as a unit had only played a few gigs. Brian and Roger had played with their band Smile, including a benefit gig at The Albert Hall. Imperial College was not a big venue and it had a small, shallow stage. I remembered shooting Chuck Berry and his duckwalk there a couple of months earlier. The significance of the Imperial College show for Queen was that it was in London, and it was sold-out. So somehow, by word of mouth they had garnered a following. And Freddie worked the audience like it was a stadium. He was already projecting huge. Already there was a certain operatic quality in his attitude.

I was immediately impressed by how sonically proficient they were even on that little stage. I mean it was tiny. You can clearly see from the images I took with the flash that there was little room for them to charge around, not that this fact stopped Freddie from making all his dramatic performance gestures and flourishes. For a band that had hardly sold a record, they were surprisingly sophisticated for all the limitations of the situation.

Freddie was physically in Imperial College, but he was projecting somewhere miles outside. The sheer size of the performance! Queen were born to be on a massive stage. A few months later that success was launched by the release of *Queen II*, their second album, and the hit single it spawned, "Seven Seas Of Rhye." From the battered van to the Top Ten... Queen had finally arrived.

One significant note I made when I first looked at these photos after rescuing them from deep in my archive, was that Freddie is using a standard mike setup. I'd completely forgotten about that, probably because these photos were hardly seen at the time. The press (or what there was of it back then) had barely registered them. By the time we did our first studio shoot, maybe a couple of weeks later, he brought with him the half-mike stand which became a trademark feature of his live performances throughout his career. And of course he's using it in all the subsequent performance images that I shot of him. I somehow had always assumed he'd had it from the start. I later learned that the bottom of the mike stand had fallen off at a performance between the Imperial College gig and our first studio session, and Freddie made it into a permanent prop.

# "...from the battered van to the top ten...Queen had finally arrived!" MR

*"...Queen had a big thing for Hendrix. They'd talk about him and Led Zeppelin and David Bowie. Freddie would specifically talk about Joni Mitchell. I remember how enamored he was with* Court And Spark *when it was first released..."* MR

IMPERIAL COLLEGE GIG NOVEMBER 1973

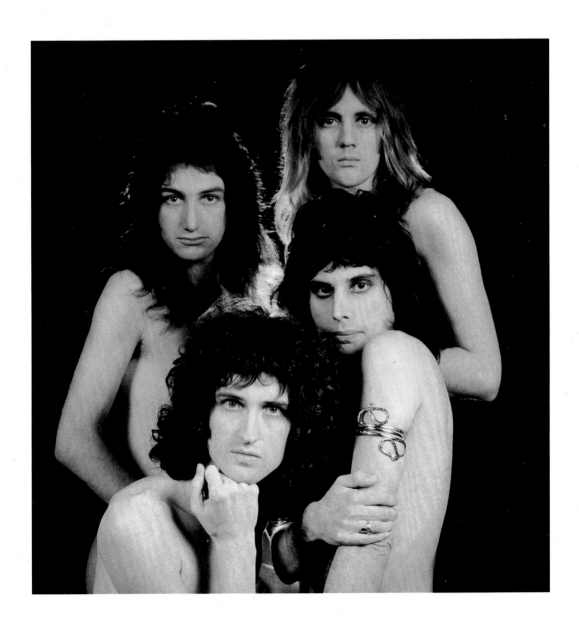

We tried a bunch of looks on that first session. One of them was a series of photos based around the "royalty" idea. The giant sceptre was Freddie's. I subsequently found out that Brian hated any images that featured any of the trappings of royalty, and that the rest of the band were just going along with it to pacify Freddie. My response to Brian was: "Let's just do them, since Freddie seems so set on it. You've got nothing to lose, since we're going to do other setups. If you really hate them, they don't have to see the light of day!" So he went along with it. And of course he really didn't like them and they never did get published at that time. All these years later they have acquired a kind of kitsch period charm, and I've come across many longtime Queen fans that really love them. The passage of time can often change how one views particular photos (but not in Brian's case, I suspect!).

Of course in many ways the "topless" shots are just as kitsch, but they were the ones that were approved by the band. They certainly fulfilled the image of "androgyny" that the band was keen to project, and they got immediate attention from the rock press, not all of it positive. Not that Freddie cared. The band was as pretty as a bunch of schoolgirls, and the photos garnered them some attention. All of that was only a good thing in Freddie's eyes, though I'm not sure that the rest of the band was so convinced! But that was why they had come to me. They wanted some of that full tilt "glam" image that I had become adept at garnering.

They knew that it was going to take something really strong to visually cut through. And so it happened that the first serious notice Queen ever attracted in the UK rock press was from these "nudie pictures." In fact, they had their trousers on, but they look like they are nude in these shots. Looking back there is certainly something over-the-top about these images. And they got some flak from the *NME* who took the piss out of them. But they published one of the pictures, and that was the most important factor.

The key thing about this session was that they wanted something sensational, an image that people would talk about. Criticism didn't matter; the most important thing was to get spoken about. It had been the same with Bowie. First of all everybody commented on his appearance, then they were playing the music. David set the blueprint of how to approach this game. They knew that it was necessary to do something visually that would catch people's attention. Queen had grasped what was needed. They got themselves some ink.

## "...they got immediate attention from the rock press, not all of it positive...that was only a good thing in Freddie's eyes, though I'm not sure that the rest of the band was so convinced..." MR

"...there was plenty of bickering, disagreement and discussion but that was part of the process. I never saw any ganging up or experienced any bad feeling. They bitched to each others' faces. They were genuinely fond of each other. They were a group and they wanted to make that super clear..." MR

"The concept of Queen is to be regal and majestic.

Glamour is part of us, **and** we want to be dandy...

and it was really the dandy thing we were into: dressing up, fooling around. Even in those days we knew we'd make it."

*Freddie Mercury {1974}*

My early impression was that politically Freddie was my best ally, for a number of reasons. Firstly, I realized that if this band was called Queen it was because Freddie and not the other three had wanted it to be called that. In fact, I remember Freddie giggling about it. They explained that it was also about being like Queen Elizabeth or Queen Victoria: magnificent. I said that it could equally have been "King" to them once but Freddie just said, "No, it's absolutely impossible. It couldn't have been King, it doesn't have the same ring or aura as Queen." Because the other three weren't gay, they were particularly keen to make sure that I understood that it also meant regal. They were a little sensitive to that but I realized that if they were prepared to go along with the name then they were prepared to go along with other things. They had a certain trust in Freddie's instincts. I grasped quickly that Freddie would be my best ally. I'd learnt previously with other bands that it was wise to find out early on who the dominant personality was, and with Queen in those early days it was the amazing Mr. Mercury.

Freddie and I had a lot of interests in common. We had a rapport. I always liked extreme personalities and he was certainly into pushing the envelope, but he was also a very sweet guy. He would often invite me to go and hang out at his place. Sometimes Mary would be there or she'd be in the other room. I thought they were such a cute pair. At times, in their little apartment he was like the Queen Mother. I would show up and he'd be wearing a dressing gown and slippers in the afternoon. He loved tea, and I still cherish those times with Freddie and his teatime chats.

He loved gossip, and it intrigued him that I knew Lou and David so well, and he certainly encouraged our friendship. He could talk for hours about so many things. He would talk about his mum a lot, whom he obviously cared greatly for. I don't really remember him talking much about his father. I think his mother was very accepting of his flamboyance; she didn't find it embarrassing as some parents at that period might have.

It was obvious to me that Freddie liked boys, but then that was the flavor of the year; you liked boys and you liked girls. The difference was that some liked boys a lot more, and Freddie clearly belonged in that category. I was married and my interest was basically girls, but I enjoyed flirting with the boys. The truth is I enjoyed the company of gay and bisexual men, who often seemed more sensitive and more creative than the average heterosexual male. I was very much a child of my times.

On the day of a photo shoot Freddie could generally persuade the others to do what he wanted. Looking like they had no clothes on was my idea, but Freddie got the others to do it. If he was a bit fifty-fifty in his attitude, they would challenge him, but if he expressed a strong desire to pursue a certain course, the others could probably be persuaded.

**"I hate pockets in trousers. By the way, I do not wear a hose. My hose is my own. No coke bottle, nothing stuffed down there."**
*Freddie Mercury {1974}*

There was a quality of innocence about Brian May that he still seems to maintain all these years later. I never got the sense that he had any particular interest in a "hip" or "alternative" lifestyle. He just seemed to want to write and play music. He was – and seems still to be – essentially eclectic, and very bright, a doctor of astronomy, with a genuine interest in collecting, including stereo photography. Also, I've been told by a publisher who is currently working with him, he's the foremost collector and archivist of all things Queen-related. He's a wild and experimental guitarist with a strong academic bent.

Brian was so much a part of the sound of Queen. But musically I think of the band as a whole. In terms of the structure of the group, I always saw some parallels with The Beatles, even though this was a much more camp group. Because they loved harmonies, Queen loved The Beatles. And just as John Lennon was a domineering personality over the younger Paul and George, the same was also true of Freddie, who was a couple of years older than anyone else. Brian, if you like, was the Paul McCartney of the piece. Just as Paul might have been a slightly junior member of The Beatles in the early days, without him there couldn't have been The Beatles. It was just the same with Brian and the influence of his unique guitar sound. Of course, from the start he was also a strong writer, just not quite as prolific as Freddie. Queen was a combination of four incredible elements. One was great songs. Two was Freddie's voice (he believed that his teeth gave him extra resonance). Three was Brian May's guitar, and four was the harmonizing.

*"...Brian always built his own guitars with his father's help. All those wild effects on the first records were recorded without synthesizers. They all came from Brian's guitar..." MR*

From the earliest days, Roger was the most geared to being a rock star; not only did he look the part but he enjoyed it. He was extremely popular with the ladies and he had an eye for them too. He was a very relaxed and easy-going guy. He was a lot of fun, and out of them all, the most comfortable socially and the most overtly charming in the classic sense.

He was quite easy to work with and would always be up for it. If I wanted him to do a bit of posing he was ready like a shot. He and Freddie were the most ready for photo sessions.

ROGER SOLO SESSION 1974

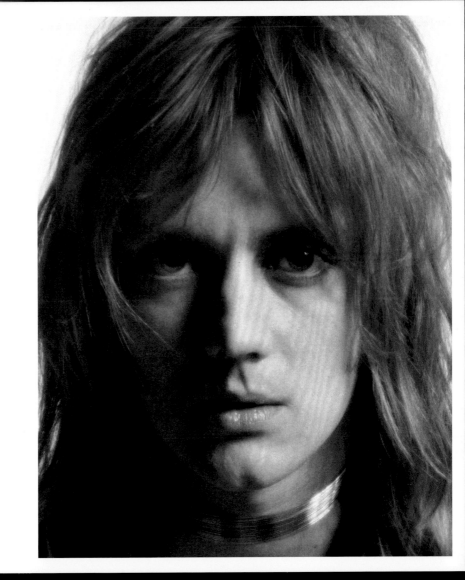

John (like George in The Beatles) was considered the "quiet" one. The other three were always chattering, scheming, bickering, laughing, and projecting, but, at least in our sessions, John was quite happy to go along with whatever the others were up for. He was a quiet, gentle person, really very easy and undemanding to deal with; a sweet soul.

He was a sort of classic bass player. Paul McCartney aside, most of them don't say a lot. Occasionally he would get talkative, but the other three were always on, like bumblebees.

Even though he was the last to join the band, and the least expressive, the others made sure to include him in on the decision-making. He clearly fitted in. From the start they told me, "It's a band. It's all four of us," even though John hadn't written anything at that point. He was clearly happy to be in the band, and if the other three wanted the theme to be black and white, then why not? In the pictures they look like a single unit. John's creative contribution developed as his confidence in his realationship with the others became stronger. At first he was just the bass player. He wasn't initially one of the harmonizers at the beginning and he didn't write any of the songs on the first two albums. But he came into his own in a big way when he wrote the classic Queen "funk" track, "Another One Bites The Dust," which was a huge Number One hit in the States.

He wasn't shy about having his picture taken. He never tried to hide or turn his head away and he was just as concerned as the others about getting his hair right! He just didn't say a lot. He never used to say anything on stage, but then he spoke to a billion people at the Freddie Mercury Tribute Concert, and I don't think he's said a public word since. Maybe the sound of his own voice at such volume scared him!

*"...what has struck me, looking at the pictures, is how often John is singing. I just thought of him as playing the bass. I never thought of him in that way. Maybe he only did when they played live..." MR*

That was the way the group functioned, as far as I could see. Freddie played the role of queen bee, but in return the other three had the right to knock him or tease him a bit. They were always joking together. The other three would lead Freddie on and he would take a certain amount of ribbing from the others, but he loved that kind of attention. Brian and Roger teased him a lot. They called him "an old tart" or "an old queen." That was just the parlance of the time. In fact, one thing about Queen is that they talked the entire time, throughout every session I did with them. Shooting Roger or Freddie on their own, was easy and a lot of fun. Shooting the four of them together was really distracting. They were bright, but they were like kookaburras.

The big impression that I got from the beginning was that these guys were very close. They certainly liked each other a lot and were very comfortable with one another. They had a definite personal bond.

The second studio session was the one that produced the image that became almost like a photo-logo for Queen. It was shot for the cover of their second album, but was recreated for the video for what would become their most acclaimed track "Bohemian Rhapsody." It certainly projects very big. I've often called it their "Four Horsemen of the Apocalypse" image! Freddie and I loved it from the start, but it took a bit of arm bending on Freddie's part to get the other three to acquiesce. They thought they might get bitten by the pretentious criticism again, which of course only fuelled Freddie's enthusiasm.

Freddie connected with Zandra Rhodes and that whole black and white theme. My brief for the cover of *Queen II* was exactly that: they wanted to feature the band and it was to be a black and white concept.

That's when I came across the Kobal Collection. I had a Canadian friend called John Kobal, who had a large collection of Hollywood stills. I connected with him. At an exhibition of his archive pictures, he suggested making an exchange. In return for me taking the liner portrait for his new book, he would give me prints from his collection. These photos included Marlene Dietrich in the film *Shanghai Express*.

Although it isn't easy to explain, I made an instant connection in my mind to Queen. It had something to do with Freddie's personality and the general aura of the group, which was something outrageous and yet at the same time magnificent. And there I was staring at the very essence of it in this movie still. I've always been up front about where I got the idea for the cover shot: Marlene Dietrich. It was unique. No other shot in my thousands of photographs was influenced in this way.

I acquired the print, and then in a secondhand shop found a book on Marlene Dietrich, which had the same shot on the cover. I bought it to show to Freddie: "Look at this. I know that this has got to be it." He knew immediately that he wanted to be Marlene, and that we'd figure everything else out around that. We talked to the rest of the group and they were interested, but they also wanted a shot where they were all dressed in white against a white background.

I wanted to get the same "hooded" shadow on all of them and this necessitated using a completely different form of lighting from normal. We had to light all four of them at the correct angle. A half inch one way or another would destroy the way the hood went over the eyes so I had to try to control them. I made a lot of little adjustments to the lighting during the shoot. Sometimes their eyes were a little less hooded and in some frames you can see the buttons on their black shirts more clearly.

The way the band was lined up for the shot seemed obvious from the start. Of course Freddie as the front man would take the "Dietrich" pose with the hands and be upfront. Brian was the tallest, but also with his hair being wild and wavy it made symmetrical sense to put him at the back. Roger and John's hair had a similar length and look, so they balanced off the image at the sides, although if you check the multitude of frames out you'll see that they have changed sides in different variations. It was all about the hair. The arrangement had no other significance. If Roger's hair had been thick and wavy and Brian's had been straight, Roger would have been at the back. We did attempt some shots with Brian with his head right back but that wasn't easy. Everyone was nervous. It was only their second ever studio photo session. The guys were still learning when it came to pictures. They fidgeted the whole time, and kept running up and down the ladder getting their hair and makeup right. They were always running back to look in the mirror. It wasn't just Freddie, they were all at it.

In the middle of this performance with the mirrors and the makeup, I would stop to do my headstands. They always joked about my yoga obsession. They found it very amusing. Freddie even liked to playfully pat my posterior while I was in an inverted position. They put a lot of work into the shoot on the day, and they were very enthusiastic to get it "right."

When we printed up the pictures they started to get a little anxious, particularly when they remembered the *NME* remarks about the topless pictures. They could see how strong the black shot was, but they were worried that it was maybe a little too strong. I could understand why they were a little sensitive: they didn't want the image to get in the way of the music.

MARLENE DIETRICH

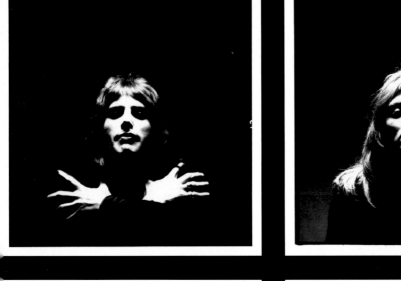

*QUEEN II* SHOOT 1973

*"...around the time of* Queen II *Freddie started giving the right sort of interviews, but of course he always had a bad time with the press; they gave him flak for being pretentious. He got given that label because he wanted nothing less than the rock 'n' roll throne. Often pretenders don't get that, but of course he and Queen, did." MR*

"To be honest, performing comes quite easily really, it doesn't take me that much. On stage I just click. I mean, I know it sounds conceited and there are a lot of setbacks and a lot of strains and nerves, but not nearly as much as there used to be. Now we are a headline band we know that people have come to see us. Being support was one of the most traumatic experiences of my life."

*Freddie Mercury {1974}*

*"...they wore their clothes well. They're all skinny and quite tall. They were a well-balanced band visually...they naturally looked like a posse of little princesses..." MR*

Previous page RAINBOW THEATRE MARCH 1974

"...they were fun and they were cute. Even without make up on they were pretty adorable, friendly people. Brian had the best hair and he always looked as though he could be straight out of an Aubrey Beardsley painting. That's why he was at the back..." MR

*QUEEN II* SHOOT 1973

Queen's gig at Imperial College had opened a lot of people's eyes, and ears, to the huge potential of the band. They were visually stunning and in Freddie Mercury they possessed the most animated front man since Mick Jagger. They also sounded like nothing and no one else. Music writers could usually find some label to stick on a band to describe their sound but with Queen it was different. More than glam and more than rock, Queen were simply Queen.

**"We're not just an average, normal rock group really, we're just very weird. We do things that people least expect, not just for the sake of just doing them but because it is just the phase we are going through."**
*Freddie Mercury {1974}*

They consolidated the success of *Queen II* and "Seven Seas Of Rhye" by touring the UK as support to Mott The Hoople; their music and performances reaching new, larger audiences and gaining them a whole set of new fans.

They all got on very well with Mott. You couldn't get more down to earth than Ian Hunter and he loved them. They all became very close on that tour. The idea of a band called "Queen" may have upset a lot of people at the time they first gained some profile, but once people got to know them they were won round. In principle Queen were very well mannered and easy to like. Freddie, especially, knew how to have fun with everybody.

The plan was to then tour the States, again with Mott The Hoople, but it was after the first successful week long stint in New York in 1974 that Brian became ill, first with hepatitis and then a duodenal ulcer. He was in hospital for about three or four months, and they had to miss most of the US tour; which was the last time they supported anyone. At the time Brian didn't seem that strong physically. He was very skinny and some people wondered if he really would be able to handle the grueling aspects of "life on the road." But obviously he turned out to be much more durable physically than many expected…

Serious though Brian's illness was, the band did what they could to begin recording a third album while he recovered in hospital. With Brian's input eventually added, the result was their most successful album to date, *Sheer Heart Attack*. A record of staggering complexity, it highlighted Brian's unique guitar sound and gave them their first massive hit "Killer Queen," a number Two in the UK in 1975. Queen were now enjoying the kind of success that their flamboyant image demanded; it was no more than they or their music deserved. Certainly in their minds!!

*"...I was always sure that Freddie was a very honorable person. I've never known him throughout any business transaction, for example, to be dishonest. He was always very accepting of others' input, always showing his appreciation. I think changes that occurred in Freddie just went with the image and the person that he then became. You see it a lot within the music business: you see others putting on an image and it's like they are writing about a character. I should think you actually get to the point where you don't like that character any more. Then you can close the book and start again. But at that point, there were at least three sides to Freddie's character. There was his past, there was the core Freddie, and there was Mercury. And it was Freddie that I enjoyed and loved. I don't think I've ever met a person who was as much fun. There was a special charm to him, an unusually intuitive intelligence..." MR*

"The kids react the way they do because at last they have found something

# completely original.
### Nothing we do is anything like what other groups are doing."

*Freddie Mercury {1971}*

"I really do love performing.
I mean,
it's natural for me.

I'm a dandy,
a show-off. I get very
high on all the attention.

I love it."

*Freddie Mercury {1974}*

Queen were starting to get some traction in the teen market, because they were so pretty. Especially Roger. He looked the part of "teen idol" better than any of them. He had this sweet, bright eyed, slightly cheeky aura, and the young girls loved it. He was very popular from the moment they garnered a little profile.

My shoot at his home was a commission from one of the many teen/rock 'n' roll fashion magazines, but I can't remember which one. So I went to the ground floor flat in the house he was renting at the time just on the outskirts of London, a modest abode, with certain bohemian rock trappings. He was very cooperative. He was quite happy to be photographed in bed, putting on his trousers, with a tea cozy on his head (his idea!), holding his cat, straddling a bicycle, whatever popped into our minds.

You can even see some fan mail from Japan on his bed. As I recall they hit it really big in Japan from the moment they set foot in Tokyo, in many ways harder and faster than even the UK. They followed in Bowie's wake, who'd also garnered feverish audiences from his first Ziggy visit to Japan, and their overt androgyny also helped get them over.

ROGER AT HOME MARCH 1974

ROGER AT HOME MARCH 1974

"The whole group is aiming for the top-slot. We're not going to be content with anything less. That's what we're striving for. It's got to be there. I definitely know we've got it in the music, we're original enough…and now we're proving it."
*Freddie Mercury {1974}*

"I'm just being my flamboyant self and having a good time. It would be so boring if everything was laid out and everybody knew what everything was all about all the time. I like people to make up their own interpretations."
    *Freddie Mercury {1975}*

"*...Freddie always got excited before a show, but maybe that's true of all great performers. Every concert was important. I must have seen 30-odd shows over that 18-month period or so. He was always very aware that each one was a new show. He wasn't merely going out to entertain, he was going out to astound. The regal thing. It was very important to him that each show should be big and should be fabulous...*" MR

"I find that even when people have let you down, you just want to go on stage. It's very gratifying to know that all sorts of people want you."
    *Freddie Mercury {1985}*

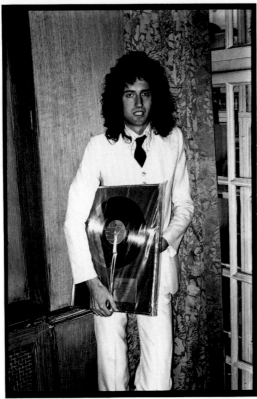

*QUEEN II* AWARDS CEREMONY CAFE ROYAL LONDON 1974. Opposite page *QUEEN II* TOUR 1974

"...he always had warmth for the audience. It was always: 'Hello darlings!' and 'My little sweeties'! He had a genuine excitement that people were there to see him. He was not laid back about it. He loved it; he was determined to deliver; he embraced it..." MR

"...sometimes the audience would sing, 'God Save The Queen' before the concert. It would really pump Freddie up. He'd be thinking that they were singing about him and only him..." MR

"My dear I'm the vainest creature going
but then so are all pop-stars..."
*Freddie Mercury {1974}*

ROGER SOLO SHOOT MAY 1974

I enjoyed working with Queen as a group. They were very bright, lively and charming when they were together, but I also really enjoyed it when it was just Freddie and me. There was an immediate empathy between us from our first meeting that shows up strongly in the solo sessions, and in many ways time has proven our sessions to have generated Freddie's most memorable solo images, and certainly the prettiest! They were more low-key and gossipy than the group sessions and of course with none of the others around I had his undivided attention, which lent a certain intensity and intimacy to the results.

We never approached these solo affairs with any particular plan or concept. Freddie got made up, and tried on different outfits and we played and riffed, and we really didn't put a foot wrong. He especially loved his red velvet jacket, which I believe he had come across in his days of running the store with Roger at Kensington market. And he was thrilled with the classic Greek-looking tunic that he had commissioned Zandra Rhodes to make for him. It was certainly "glam" and androgynous, but also a little space age. As I recall the tunic had been finished only a couple of days beforehand, so he was thrilled to give it its first airing at our session. I shot him in it against white and black backgrounds, in keeping with the black/white theme that was important to his and the band's early image. It was just such a spectacular and unique piece of work, and gave endless possibilities to our image making. Freddie was delighted when he saw the results (as indeed was I).

*"...when Freddie was pumped up, he was really pumped up. But when he was relaxed, he was like a sister. He had the ability to make you feel intimate with him very easily. It was the way he would talk, he'd love to giggle. He'd make gestures with his fingers and his mouth too. He was very warm. But when he was going to go on stage he would be almost like another person...Freddie wasn't being pretentious; he could deliver. It was always the dumbest accusation to level against him. It is only ever pretentious if you can't deliver..." MR*

**"I'm a man of extremes. I have a soft side and a hard side with not a lot in between. If the right person finds me I can be very vulnerable, a real baby, which is invariably when i get trodden on. But sometimes, I'm hard, and when I'm strong no one can get to me."**
*Freddie Mercury {1974}*

FREDDIE SOLO SHOOT JUNE 1974

FREDDIE SOLO SHOOT JUNE 1974

*"...Freddie always came to the sessions with a lot of different outfits, he was always very game. He didn't need much encouragement. He wore a couple of jackets quite often; a maroony crushed velvet one was one of his favorites. He was always very fin de siecle. He was very much into being a dandy. The loose jackets and tight trousers – and his body language.*

*He needed a little direction in front of the cameras because he was somewhat self-conscious about his teeth. So I wouldn't thunder on like I did with some people; I took a little time so that he would feel composed about his facial expressions. We would discuss it and we actually worked together on his expressions so that he could keep his mouth closed and also suck his cheeks in a bit. He'd ask me how he looked and I'd direct him and say, 'A little bit more of this, that way...' He looked pretty damn good generally. I didn't think his teeth looked bad with his mouth open but he specifically didn't want that. He'd always say to me, 'Look Mick, watch my mouth.' I talked to him about getting his teeth done, but he never would because he thought that it would affect his voice. He had an extra four teeth at the back which pushed the other teeth forward..."* MR

FREDDIE SOLO SHOOT JUNE 1974

"People think I'm an ogre at times. Some girls hissed at me in the street,

'You devil!' They think they we're really nasty, but that's only on stage. Off stage, well I'm certainly not an ogre." *Freddie Mercury {1974}*

"People are apprehensive when they meet me. They think I'm going to eat them.

But underneath it all I'm quite shy."

*Freddie Mercury {1977}*

FREDDIE SOLO SHOOT DECEMBER 1974

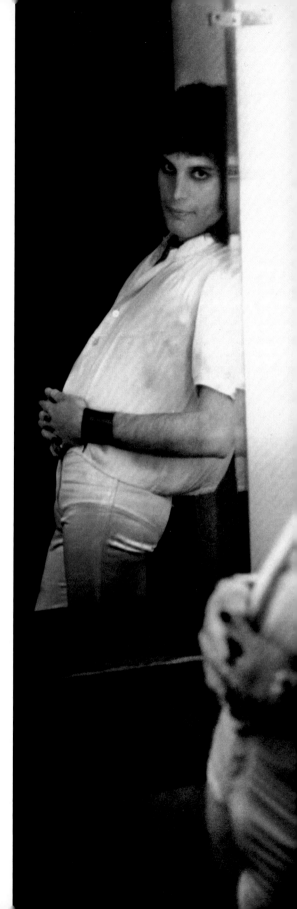

RAINBOW THEATRE NOVEMBER 1974

Following page FREDDIE SOLO SHOOT JUNE 1974

"...during the time I was around the band, I didn't ever see Freddie's hard side. I honestly never saw him being mean to anyone. He was very strong but I would never call him hard. He was just outrageously camp, and not everybody could deal with that...one time a fan I had met through Bowie wanted to meet Freddie. After a gig I took him backstage and introduced them. I don't know if the kid loved the music or just was in love with Freddie, but he got blind drunk, and basically threw up all over Freddie's shoes. Freddie was very understanding about the whole thing. He took the shoes off and told the kid not to worry, and was actually being very caring about him, getting some water, looking for some bicarbonate of soda. I mean, the kid had thrown up all over his shoes! Freddie was walking around in his bare feet, but was definitely much more concerned about the young man's well being than he was about his shoes..." MR

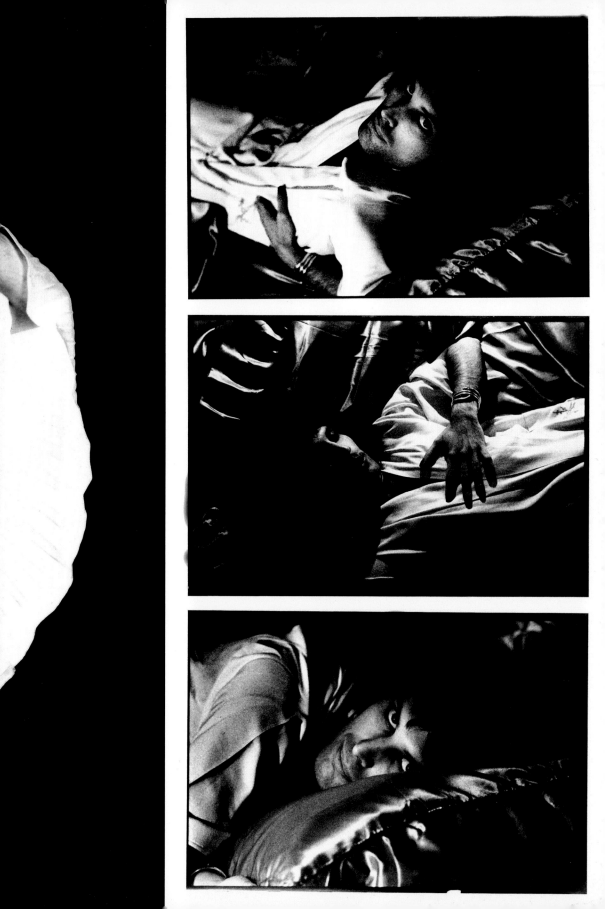

FREDDIE SOLO SHOOT DECEMBER 1974. Following page RAINBOW THEATRE NOVEMBER 1974

You can see how close Mary and Freddie were from the photos I took of them, both the ones backstage at the Rainbow Theatre and the frames I shot that day in my studio. She was essentially a very shy and modest girl, who was quite happy for Freddie to be the centre of attention and only agreed to do the photos with a little reluctance to please Freddie. Freddie and Mary… Their names went together in the minds of their friends. They were a definite couple and were clearly in love. I'm glad she agreed to let me take them, because I don't think I've seen any other pictures of the two of them together. There probably are others, but I've never seen them. And of course, when he died, Freddie willed his estate to her, so, whatever other relationships he was subsequently involved with, she clearly never left his heart. I've seen an interview clip from the 80s where he says that she is the only person in his life that he totally trusted…

FREDDIE SOLO SHOOT WITH MARY AUSTIN JUNE 1974         **139**

*"...maybe Mary brought the clothes along for Freddie's session, and that's perhaps why she's in some of the pictures. Or maybe they simply said to me, 'Oh, we'd love some pictures of the two of us.' It makes sense. I mean, I've done that at other times..."* MR

"I remember back in an interview where I said, 'I play on the bisexual thing.' Of course I play on it. It's simply a matter of wherever my mood takes me. If people ask me if I'm gay, I tell them it's up to them to find out."
*Freddie Mercury {1976}*

The band was on a serious roll and their profile had risen rapidly in the wake of the success of "Seven Seas of Rhye" (their first hit single). They needed some new images for promotion, so this session was quickly scheduled. We didn't really know what we wanted to do. We just jumped in and experimented with several setups, which we quickly discarded. You can see this from the number of test Polaroids. I'm not sure why we didn't carry these setups to filmic fruition; they look pretty good to me from the perspective of today. But anyway we hit a groove that we all liked and got on with things. They wanted something more casual, less stylized. The rest of the band wanted to tone down the androgyny image and just make it more straight-ahead rock 'n' roll, and this time Freddie went along with it.

Opposite page HAMMERSMITH ODEON DECEMBER 1975. This page PHOTO SESSION AUGUST 1974

"...in many of the pictures in this book, the band are smiling, and especially so in this session; here they are fooling around and laughing. These images were press shots. They would have turned up on packages, like foreign singles. Queen are less stylized and more relaxed than in our earlier sessions. I was obviously looking for ideas because there are Polaroids of setups that I experimented with but never shot. We went into this session without any clear ideas. They wanted something a little less controlled and not so overtly glam, although they are pretty glam still. But this is much looser than the earlier sessions. The rolls that they are leaning against, in the next images are scene backdrops rolled up..." MR

This page PHOTO SESSION AUGUST 1974
Opposite page *SHEER HEART ATTACK* ALBUM COVER SESSION SEPTEMBER 1974

"God, the agony we went through to have the pictures taken, dear. Can you imagine trying to convince the others to cover themselves in Vaseline and then have a hose turned on them? Everyone was expecting some sort of cover. A *Queen III* cover really, but this is completely new. It's not that we're changing altogether. We're still the same dandies we started out to be. We're just showing people we're not merely a load of old poofs, that we are capable of other things."

*Freddie Mercury {1974}*

I can't remember whether the pictures that finally became the *Sheer Heart Attack* album cover were early on or late in the shoot, but there are a lot of different looks in those shots. Some are quite dark, some have a certain bluish color to them, but they are basically the same set. They all look very tanned for these photos, so they must have just come back from a well-earned rest in the sun! *Sheer Heart Attack* was different from the *Queen II* cover because the band was much clearer about what they wanted. It was their idea for me to create a "wasted" look, washed up on some far away shore, soaked and greasy. They came to me with a specific brief, "We want to look abandoned, like we've been marooned on a desert island." They wanted really bold lettering on the front. I was the art director as well as the photographer, but they knew exactly what they wanted and they were much more confident in their opinions. It was their concept. They wanted to make that point and by this stage they were getting more control over everything. Well, they got what they wanted, but as their statements about this shoot have made me aware over the years I think what they got was a little more than they bargained for

With *Queen II*, I had directed the shoot until I got to the point where I was happy with it, but with *Sheer Heart Attack* they looked at the Polaroids and made suggestions. Some of these were specific and deliberate and, as is the case with most pictures, some of it was intuitive between the parties involved. I always feed off what comes to me during the photo session. I don't even pose things too heavily; I go for what the moment suggests. That's why I tried out those different backgrounds and played around with backlighting.

They brought their own clothes. I got the sprays, glycerin, and Vaseline, and we greased them up and then spritzed them. They lay on the floor for a couple of hours and as much as they felt uncomfortable they didn't complain. Which was just as well, because it was their idea!! I just kept shooting until I was done. The makeup girl had to keep a close eye on the eye makeup so that it didn't run. We had to keep stopping and starting and respraying. It did go on for a while, though maybe not as long as their distinct discomfort has made them think it was. It wasn't as if they begged to quit the setup. We both had very thorough attitudes. I shot it in a number of ways, all the time stopping for more test Polaroids, and a little more Vaseline and water spray. Whatever it took! One thing was for sure we had to get it right first time because I was quite aware that nobody in their right mind would be prepared to suffer for this particular piece of art a second time!

They were now starting to get more of a look. They were looking a little more mature and feeling more confident by this time. They had had a hit single, "Seven Seas of Rhye," *Queen II* had had some success, they were doing well in America, and it was obvious that something had started to happen. They were still glamorous but they had a more mature kind of glamour, not quite as overt as in some of the earlier pictures.

## "...they brought their own clothes. I got the sprays, glycerin, and Vaseline, and we greased them up and then spritzed them..." MR

PHOTO SESSION AUGUST 1974

*SHEER HEART ATTACK* ALBUM COVER SESSION SEPTEMBER 1974          **153**

"We tend to work well under pressure. But do we row?
Oh my dear we're the bitchiest band on earth. You'll
have to spend a couple of days with us. We're at each
other's throats! But if we didn't agree we'd just be
yes-men, and we do get the cream in the end."
*Freddie Mercury {1974}*

From the start Queen delivered very big and consistently in performance. Freddie especially loved an audience, and he was a fantastic performer and front man from that first Imperial College gig that I saw. I never saw him have an off night. Show him an audience and he was ready. This was more than naked ambition or attention mongering. He genuinely adored his audience and fed off their enthusiasm for his art and talent. The passage of time has proven him to be one of the great popular entertainers of all time: for his divine voice, his brilliant songwriting, and the overwhelming exuberance of his live performances. This rocker had it all, and then some…

I was fortunate enough to see the Queen audience grow in size and enthusiasm before my eyes, although there's no way I could have imagined quite how massive their popularity would become. Even Freddie once told me hanging out after a gig I saw them play Madison Square Garden in New York in the early eighties, that as sure as he always was that they would become significant, he found the level of their success a little overwhelming at times (but he still loved it!)

HAMMERSMITH ODEON DECEMBER 1975

"I do all the leaping about, but that's what singers should do now. The sound comes from all of us:

Queen work together as a unit."

*Freddie Mercury {1974}*

"I was caught up in being a star and I thought, 'This is the way a star behaves'. Now I don't give a damn. I want to do things my way and have fun. If all my money ended tomorrow, I'd still go about like I had lots of money because that's what I used to do before. I'll always walk round like a Persian Popinjay and no one's gonna stop me. I love living life to the full – that's my nature.

Nobody tells me what to do."
*Freddie Mercury {1985}*

"We're probably the fussiest band in the world, to be honest. We take so much care with what we do because we feel so much about what we put across. And if we do an amazing album we make sure that album is packaged right, because we've put so much loving into it."

*Freddie Mercury {1975}*

"...Freddie and Brian would have dinner with their crew. They were good like that, they were pretty democratic. They would eat with the roadies and drivers. As much as they were magnificent and uninterested in the mundane, they didn't treat anybody as if they were less worthy because they weren't fabulously talented or absolutely whacked out. The pictures of me alone and with Mary were taken by Freddie..." MR

"We want to give value for money. There are things we want to put across. We don't want people to think of us just as a hard, basic rock band, because we can do more than that...If you see us up on a stage, that's what we're all about. We are basically a rock band. All the lights and the paraphernalia are only there to enhance what we do."

*Freddie Mercury {1974}*

LIVE 1975

TRIDENT STUDIOS WITH EDDIE HOWELL AUGUST 1975 (continued on following page)

LIVE 1975

"I like an audience to respond. Maybe we'd like them to sit down and listen to some songs but I get a lot more from them when they're going wild, and it brings more out of me."
  *Freddie Mercury {1974}*

By 1975, Queen were on the verge of what they'd been born for: superstardom. *Sheer Heart Attack* and "Killer Queen," the single taken from it had established them in the forefront of the modern rock acts. *Sheer Heart Attack* had reached the Top Ten in the States. They followed it with a world tour and then, in late 1975, with what many regard as their magnum opus, *A Night At The Opera*.

It was an album that broke new ground in every direction, not least in that the first single taken from the album was the six-minute long "Bohemian Rhapsody," a rock operetta, which went to the top of the UK charts and simply stayed there for what seemed like forever. They also made their first music video to promote it, based around the image I had directed and conceived for their *Queen II* album cover. And Queen weren't just dominating the singles chart; for a sizeable part of 1976, all the band's first four albums were amongst the UK's Top Twenty.

Then they were off on another world tour which culminated in September 1976 with a free concert in Hyde Park which attracted a crowd of almost 200,000. It also coincided with the release of *A Day At The Races*, their most successful album to that point. The band then toured the USA and Europe again before another album followed in 1977, News Of The World, which contained the anthemic hits "We Will Rock You," and "We Are The Champions," which were intended by Freddie to be stadium chants and promptly became just that.

Following that was always going to be tricky but the band managed it with *Jazz* in 1978, not least because it featured a photo of a female nude bike race on the cover. Another tour followed and then the live album *Live Killers*, which went some way to capturing the pomp of a Queen concert on record.

The band then turned their hands to film, providing an unforgettable soundtrack to the movie Flash Gordon. But by this point there really wasn't much the band couldn't do. *The Game* topped the charts all over the world in 1980 and the point was underlined when the single "Another One Bites The Dust" went to Number One in the US rock, soul and disco charts simultaneously.

Soon after, the band paused briefly to draw a collective breath, and then took a couple of years to pursue solo projects, their place at the top of the pile and their place in rock history assured. They would return more popular than ever in the 1980s but the first, brilliant, and most innovative phase of their career was over.

**"We've always put our necks on the line. We did it with *Queen II*. On that album we did so many outrageous things that people started to say, 'self-indulgent crap, too many vocals, too many everything'. But that is Queen. After that they all seemed to realise that that was what Queen are all about."**
*Freddie Mercury {1975}*

"...during the early to middle Seventies, no one spent a lot of time talking about their past. I wasn't telling people I went to Cambridge. Freddie was more interested in how cute the person was or how fabulous or great a piece of art was, or in music. Our conversation centered around things like that. I don't think we were as shrink-orientated then. I know something happened after 'Bohemian Rhapsody' and Freddie became very hyper, but I don't ever recall him being temperamental. The difference between Freddie before being a star and after becoming one was very little, because he always acted like he was one..." MR

I never imagined myself as a photographer in my formative years. I was inspired by my subjects, not by the work of any other photographer. It was the rockers themselves (or at least certain ones) that turned me on photographically. If rock music hadn't come along I doubt I would have pursued the course that my life took. I never studied photography. I was never interested in technique. I just wanted to get at certain imagery. From the moment I took up a camera I found the images just flowed from my lens. I look at the *Madcap Laughs* period of my Syd Barrett photos in 1969, when I had only been taking photos for about six months, and it's clear in retrospect that I'm simply doing what I was meant to be doing, although I certainly didn't realize it in those very early days. I always felt the average monkey could take a photo. Point, focus and click… How hard can that be? But maybe not everyone's pulse and perceptions become as quickened as mine when I look through the viewfinder and the magic process begins…

Once you're in front of my lens I am in love with you, you have my total undivided attention. It doesn't matter who you are. The fact of the act is enough. Whether the shoot is for love or money (or both!) I retain a residue of affection for everyone who has ever graced my lens. That's not to say that I want to repeat the experience with every subject! But there have been a few that I've loved to do the photo dance with on repeated occasion, whether with Syd Barrett, Bowie, Lou Reed or Debbie Harry in those early days or modern subjects such as Franz Ferdinand, the Killers, the YeahYeahYeahs, and the Scissor Sisters. And for those couple of key years so long ago now when we produced so many memorable images together, I was always delighted to have Queen as a group or as individuals as the recipients of my undivided photographic attention. They certainly rocked me…

**MICK ROCK**
New York City, February 2007

# CHRONOLOGY 1970–1975

## 1970

The first Queen concerts call in local favors, flitting between Roger Taylor's hometown, Brian May's college and Freddie Mercury's Ibex contacts.

**27 June** Truro, Cornwall
The very first Queen concert. It is billed as Smile – publicity had been arranged earlier by Roger Taylor's mother – and the bass player is Mike Grose.

**12 July** Imperial College, London
First use of "Queen" on promotional posters.

**18 July** Imperial College, London
Freddie's design of the word "Queen" first appears on tickets.

**25 July** Truro, Cornwall
Mike Grose's last gig: "I was getting tired of playing, I wanted to get a 'proper' job".

**23 August** Imperial College, London
Barry Mitchell on bass: "Just before the gig Freddie suggested we all wear women's clothes! It didn't happen, thank God." Freddie's clothes are supplied by dressmaker friend Wendy and the audience is served homemade popcorn and apple juice at half time

**4 September** Swiss Cottage private school

**18 September**
Freddie and Roger close their Kensington Market stall in memory of Jimi Hendrix. They play "Voodoo Chile" at that night's rehearsal.

**16 October** College of Estates Management Hall, London

**30 October** College of Technology, St Helens
Arranged by ex-Ibex manager Ken Testi.

**31 October** Cavern Club, Liverpool

**14 November** Balls Park College, Hertford

**5 December** Shoreditch College, Surrey

**18 December** College of Technology, St Helens

**19 December** Congregational Church Hall, St Helens

## 1971

**8 January** Marquee Club, London

**9 January** Technical College, Ewell, Surrey
Queen and Genesis on the bill. Barry Mitchell's last gig.

**19 February** Hornsey Town Hall, London
New bass player "Doug" debuts

**20 February** Kingston Polytechnic, London
In front of many friends in the audience, Doug's performance detracts from the rest of the show. He is fired.

**2 July** Surrey College, Surrey
John Richard Deacon's first performance with Queen. From this day until Queen's final gig at Knebworth in 1986, their line-up will remain unchanged, augmented only occasionally by additional players.

**11 July** Imperial College, London
More popcorn from Brian's kitchen in Queensgate Terrace. John Anthony is in the audience.

Roger enrolls for a biology degree at the North London Polytechnic.

**17 July** The Garden, Penzance, Cornwall
The first of an eleven-date tour of Cornwall, arranged by Roger. The concerts are billed as "Roger Taylor and Queen" in order to cash in on local interest. One venue hails "LEGENDARY CORNISH DRUMMER ROGER TAYLOR and his band Queen".

**19 July** Rugby Club, Hayle, Cornwall

**24 July** Young Farmers' Club, Wadebridge, Cornwall

**29 July** The Garden, Penzance, Cornwall

**31 July** City Hall, Truro, Cornwall

**2 August** Rugby Club, Hayle, Cornwall

**9 August** Driftwood Spars, St Agnes, Cornwall

**12 August** Tregye Hotel, Truro, Cornwall

**14 August** NCO's mess, RAF Culdrose, Truro, Cornwall

**17 August** City Hall, Truro, Cornwall

**21 August** Carnon Downs Festival, Tregye, Cornwall

**September**
Brian's friend Terry Yeadon invites Queen to road test the new equipment at Wembley's De Lane Lea studios. The band is free to use the studios for their own purposes in the downtime. Five songs are recorded over a period of months for a demo: "Liar" (formerly Ibex's "Lover,") "Great King Rat," "The Night Comes Down," "Jesus," and "Keep Yourself Alive." Louie Austin produces/engineers. The version of "The Night Comes Down" is good enough to be used on the first Queen album.

**6 October** Imperial College, London
Industry bookers and VIPs invited. Nothing comes of it. Set list includes "Liar," "Doin' All Right," "Son and Daughter," "Jesus," "Keep Yourself Alive," (all will appear on the first album), "Hangman" (a Freddie composition that is never released), "Stone Cold Crazy" (an old Wreckage song, reworked by Queen and eventually released on *Sheer Heart Attack*) and "Jailhouse Rock".

**December**
Producers John Anthony and Roy Thomas Baker visit De Lane Lea to reconnoiter the facilities. They are impressed by Queen performing "Keep Yourself Alive" in the studio and recommend them to production company Trident.

**9 December** Swimming baths, Epsom, Surrey

**31 December** Rugby Club, Twickenham, London

## 1972

The big break. Or not. Queen only perform five concerts in this year but a lot of effort is put into studio work at Trident and hunting that elusive record deal. As with De Lane Lea, Trident allows Queen carte blanche at their studios – but only when other artists have left. "They would call us up and say, 'David Bowie's finished a few hours early so you've got from 03.00 to 07.00 when the cleaners come in to do a bit,'" recalls Brian.

**28 January** Bedford College, London
Arranged by John Deacon. Six paying customers attend.

**10 March** King's College Hospital, London
Freddie's handwritten set list from this gig shows they performed "Great King Rat" (Mercury), "See What A Fool I've Been" (Queen), and "Bama Lama Bama Loo" alongside usual numbers.

**24 March** Forest Hill Hospital, London
Trident co-owner Barry Sheffield sees the band for the first time. He is impressed.

Producer Robin Cable enlists Freddie, Brian and Roger to help on two "Spectoresque" songs he's producing, "I Can Hear Music," and "Going Back".

**June**
John graduates with a first class honors degree in electronics and begins work on his MSc; Roger earns a degree in biology.

**September**
Trident agrees to pay each band member £20 per week.

**1 November**
Queen sign up to Trident. Trident agrees to get the best record deal for their act. American Jack Nelson is employed to promote the band to the major labels.

**6 November** Pheasantry Club, London

**20 December** Marquee Club, London

## 1973

Queen's first LP, Queen, is finally completed in January, but there is no record company to release it. "It took me over a year to get Queen a deal," Nelson recalls. "Everyone turned them down".

**5 February** Langham 1 Studio, London
Queen record their first session for the BBC. "My Fairy King" suffers in the short studio time, and "Liar" features extra Freddie ad-libs, but "Keep Yourself Alive," and the May/Staffell composition from their Smile days, "Doin' All Right" are both replicated as recorded for the album.

**15 February**
Queen's BBC session is broadcast on John Peel's Radio One show as part of the Sounds of the Seventies series.

**March**
As a direct result of the BBC sessions, Queen are signed by an excited EMI for their new EMI label.

**9 April** Marquee Club, London
The first appearance of "Father to Son," a track later to appear on Queen II.

**June**
The songs Freddie, Brian and Roger had recorded with Robin Cable in 1972 are released under the name "Larry Lurex" – a direct spoof of glam sensation Gary Glitter. They fail to chart.

**6 July**
"Keep Yourself Alive" / "Son and Daughter" is released as a single in the UK. Both are Brian May compositions. Reviews were generally favorable: "A raucous, well built single" (*Record Mirror*); "New male rock band called Queen will blow your head off with a diabolical, high energy nerve tingler" (*Daily Mirror*); "If these guys look half as good as they sound they could be huge" (*NME*); "Some pleasing guitar and synthesizer work" (John Peel in *Sounds*). The song is rejected five times from the Radio One play list.

**13 July**
Queen's debut album, three years in the making, is finally released. Both Roger's suggested title *Top Fax, Pix and Info* and Roy Thomas Baker's *Deary Me* are rejected for the eponymous *Queen*.

"Keep Yourself Alive" (May
"Doin' All Right" (May/Staffell)
"Great King Rat" (Mercury)
"My Fairy King" (Mercury)
"Liar" (Mercury)
"The Night Comes Down" (May)
"Modern Times Rock 'N' Roll" (Taylor)
"Son and Daughter" (May)
"Seven Seas of Rhye" (Mercury)

"Doin' All Right" was one of the few Queen songs to feature Brian on piano. On the version later released on *Queen at the Beeb*, Roger sings the final verse.

"My Fairy King" is the obvious precursor of *Queen II*'s "March of the Black Queen" and later "Bohemian Rhapsody".

Its visual world of dragons and Samson create, Freddie claimed, the first hint of his fictional land of Rhye.

A line about "Mother Mercury" is said to have inspired his own name change. "This was the first time we'd really seen Freddie working at his full capacity," Brian recalls. "In the studio was the first chance Freddie had to do his piano things and we actually got that sound of the piano and the guitar working for the first time which was very exciting." "My Fairy King" was the first of these sort of epics where there were lots voice overdubs and harmonies.

The opening four lines draw heavily on Robert Browning's "Pied Piper of Hamlyn," replicating his ideas of "fallow deer," "honey bees have lost their stings," and "horses are born with eagle wings".

"Liar" started out as the Ibex song "Lover".

Even though the band re-recorded their De Lane Lea demos, in the end they used the version of "The Night Comes Down" pieced together at the Wembley studio.

Written and sung by Roger as most of his compositions would be. Compared by *Rolling Stone* to "Communication Breakdown".

Freddie had not finished "Seven Seas of Rhye" so a short instrumental version is included.

The Freddie track "Mad the Swine" is recorded but not included due to an argument between Queen and producer Baker over percussion sounds.

John Deacon appears as "Deacon John" on the album sleeve.

A picture taken by friend Doug Puddifoot and distorted for the cover is used only on the back. A shot of Freddie on stage is chosen instead.

The phrase "no synthesizers" appears on the album. A similar message would appear on every LP until 1980.

**Reviews**

"A thrusting, dynamic, forceful, not to mention heavy debut" – *Time Out*

"There's no doubt that this funky, energetic English quartet has all the tools they'll need to lay claim to the Zep's abdicated heavy-metal throne, and beyond that to become a truly influential force in the rock world. Their debut album is superb" – *Rolling Stone*

"Freddie Mercury is liquid heaviness. His friend Brian is an absolute dear" – *Melody Maker*

"Good listening is guaranteed in songs like 'Keep Yourself Alive,' 'Great King Rat' and 'Doin' All Right'" – *Chicago Herald*

"With its first album, Queen has produced a driving, high energy set which in time may be looked upon with the same reverence *Led Zep I* now receives" – *Winnipeg Free Press*

**13 July** Queen Mary College, Basingstoke, Hampshire
"Ogre Battle" from *Queen II* is added to the set list.

**24 July**
Unaware who the track is by, BBC's *The Old Grey Whistle Test* plays "Keep Yourself Alive" to pictures from President Roosevelt's election campaign.

**25 July** Langham 1 Studio, London
The band record "See What a Fool I've Been," "Liar," "Son and Daughter," and "Keep Yourself Alive" in their second BBC session.

**August**
Queen return to Trident studios to begin work on their second album. For the first time they are booked in as proper clients. The entire record is finished within the month. Several tracks are recorded that will never appear: John Deacon's first song "Fly by Night," Brian's "Deep Ridge" and Freddie's "Surrender to the City." Initial work on "Brighton Rock" (*Sheer Heart Attack*) and "The Prophet's Song" (*Night at the Opera*) is begun.

**9 August** Shepperton Studios
Queen are filmed for the first time miming to "Liar" and "Keep Yourself Alive".

**13 August**
"See What a Fool I've Been," "Liar," "Son and Daughter" broadcast on the BBC's Sounds of the Seventies.

**September**
Brian takes a part-time job as a teacher in Stockwell, London. He continues work on his thesis. Roger appears on Al Stewart's *Past, Present and Future* album at Trident.

**4 September**
Queen released in the United States. It charts at 83.

**13 September** Golders Green Hippodrome, London
An instrumental tape opens the show. It is called "Procession" and will be the first track of the next album. The show is recorded by the BBC for their *In Concert* series.

**24 September**
The BBC version of "Keep Yourself Alive" broadcast.

**October**
Queen request a meeting with Mick Rock to discuss their next album. "I was being interviewed," he recalls. He is played tracks from what will be *Queen II*.

**9 October**
"Keep Yourself Alive" released in the USA.

**13 October** Underground Club, Bonn, Germany
Queen's very first show outside the UK. The usual rock 'n' roll medley encore features "Big Spender".

**14 October** Le Blow Up Club, Luxembourg
Intended to be recorded but the BBC equipment fails.

**20 October** Paris Theatre, London
Recorded by the BBC. The Golders Green concert is broadcast this night.

**26 October** Imperial College, London

**November** Great Newport Street, London
Queen's first ever photo shoot with Mick Rock at his new studio. The "scepter" and "nude" pix emerge.

**2 November** Imperial College, London
Tickets from the night show prices set at 30p (including 10% VAT). Mick Rock attends to photograph. "They had played the music to me at that first meeting," he says. "I knew what I had to expect. Live they were very proficient." Freddie's microphone stand is a normal full size one.

**12 November** Town Hall, Leeds
The start of Queen's five-week, 25-date tour supporting current chart favorites Mott the Hoople. "Stone Cold Crazy" is dropped from the set list. "Modern Times Rock 'N' Roll" starts to become the second encore.

**13 November** St George's, Blackburn

**15 November** Gaumont, Worcester

**16 November** University, Lancaster

**17 November** Stadium, Liverpool

**18 November** Victoria Hall, Hanley, Staffordshire

**19 November** Civic, Wolverhampton

**20 November** New Theatre, Oxford

**21 November** Guildhall, Preston, Lancashire

**22 November** City Hall, Newcastle

**23 November** Apollo Theatre, Glasgow

**25 November** Caley Cinema, Edinburgh

**26 November** Opera House, Manchester
Mick Rock surprises Queen with a visit to discuss his concept for their next album. He has with him a photograph of Marlene Dietrich in a striking pose. He wants to replicate it on the sleeve of *Queen II* with Freddie in the role of the screen diva.

**27 November** Town Hall, Birmingham

**28 November** Brangwyn Hall, Swansea

**29 November** Colston Hall, Bristol

**30 November** Winter Gardens, Bournemouth

**1 December** Kursaal, Southend, Essex
Freddie, Roger and Brian join Mott the Hoople onstage for their encore of "All the Young Dudes".

**2 December** Central, Chatham, Kent

**3 December** Langham 1 Studio, London
Queen record again for the BBC: "Ogre Battle," "Great King Rat," Modern Times Rock 'N' Roll' and "Son and Daughter." Roger's song features a new line: "It's not that I'm bright, just happy-go-lucky".

**6 December** Cheltenham College, Cheltenham
A solo Queen show.

John Peel's *Sounds of the Seventies* broadcasts the Queen session.

**7 December** University, Liverpool
A solo Queen show.

**14 December** Hammersmith Odeon, London
Mott and Queen play two shows each although Mott overrun, cutting short the support slot. It is Queen's biggest audience (3,500), among them Brian's parents for the first time, who are asked for their autographs by eager fans.

**15 December** University, Leicester

**21 December** County Hall, Taunton, Somerset

**22 December** Town Hall, Peterborough
The final date with Mott the Hoople.

**28 December** Top Rank, Liverpool
The last show of the year, appearing on the same bill as 10cc and local band Great Day – which featured several of Freddie's Ibex bandmates.

**1974**
**January**
Voted third in *Sounds'* Best New British Band category. Brian develops a fever and a gangrenous, swollen arm in reaction to his travel injections for their forthcoming Australian trip. The band visits Mick Rock's studio in Great Newport Street again to pose for the "black" and "white" covers for their second album.

**28 January**
Queen fly to Melbourne to take part in the Sunbury Music Festival.

**2 February** Sunbury Music Festival, Melbourne
Queen's lighting rig is sabotaged, Freddie has an ear infection and Brian's arm causes him pain. The compère doesn't help with his introduction: "We've got another load of limey bastards here tonight and they're probably going to be useless..."

**February**
*NME* readers vote Queen second Most Promising New Name – despite no hits to their name.

**14 February**
An edited version of "Liar" is released in America.

**19 February**
Top of the Pops producer Robin Nash calls Queen's promoter to announce David Bowie has pulled out of the next day's recording – did he have an act that could replace him? Queen rush to record a backing tape for use on the program.

**20 February** Ramport Studios, London
Queen enter the BBC studios to pre-record a performance of "Seven Seas of Rhye".

**21 February**
"Seven Seas of Rhye" is broadcast on BBC1. Queen watch the performance on a television in an electrical shop. Panic starts, as "Seven Seas of Rhye" is not yet released as a single.

**23 February**
After one of the speediest pressings to date, EMI release Queen's second single, "Seven Seas of Rhye" / "See What a Fool I've Been." The *NME* is impressed: "This single showcases all their power and drive, their writing talents, and every quality that makes them unique".

**March**
Queen begin their first UK headlining tour, taking in 22 performances. Freddie has commissioned designer Zandra Rhodes to create their stage costumes. During this hectic month Roger finds time to pose for a solo photo shoot at his London flat.

**1 March** Winter Gardens, Blackpool
"White Queen (As It Began)" from their second album is played.

**2 March** Friars, Aylesbury, Buckinghamshire
Brian's arm hurts and the show ends early.

**3 March** Guildhall, Plymouth
At the end of the show the crowd spontaneously sings "God Save the Queen" – this becomes a tradition and Queen eventually record it for their fourth album.

**4 March** Festival Hall, Paignton, Devon

**8 March** Locarno, Sunderland
*Queen II* is released in the UK and reaches Number 5. Suggested alternative titles include *Over the Top*. Its success enables the first album to re-chart at Number 24.

"Procession" (May)
"Father to Son" (May)
"White Queen (As It Began)" (May)
"Some Day One Day" (May)
"The Loser in the End" (Taylor)
"Ogre Battle" (Mercury)
"The Fairy Feller's Master-Stroke" (Mercury)
"Nevermore" (Mercury)
"Funny How Love Is" (Mercury)
"Seven Seas of Rhye"(Mercury)

Instead of Side A and Side B, the album features Side White and Side Black.

"No synthesizers" again appears.

Written during his Smile years, "White Queen" was never performed by Staffell et al.

"Some Day One Day" is the first complete Brian vocal.

Roger again sings his track, "Loser in the End".

"Ogre Battle" was written by Freddie in 1972.

"Fairy Feller's Master-Stroke" was inspired by a painting of the same name by Richard Dadd. Freddie played harpsichord and Roy Thomas Baker the castanets. It is never performed live.

"The March of the Black Queen" continues stylistically where "My Fairy King" ended. It possibly incorporates Freddie's "Surrender to the City".

"Funny How Love Is" was written in the studio and produced using Robin Cable's "wall of sound." It is never performed live.

"Seven Seas of Rhye" ends with a chorus of "I do Like to be Beside the Seaside".

John Deacon appears under his real name.

## Reviews
"Queen is a reasonably talented band who have chosen their models unwisely … the album remains a floundering and sadly unoriginal affair" – *Rolling Stone*

"It's hard to believe that this over-produced monstrosity really was recorded by the same band which produced Queen, a genuine package of dynamite which exploded on unsuspecting heavy metal addicts on both sides of the Atlantic" – *Winnipeg Free Press*

"It's reputed Queen have enjoyed some success in the States; it's currently in the

balance whether they'll really break through here. If they do, then I'll have to eat my hat or something. Maybe Queen try too hard, there's no depth of sound or feeling" – *Melody Maker*

"Simply titled *Queen II*, this album captures them in their finest hours"– *Sounds*

"The material, performance, recording and even artwork standards are very high" – *Disc*

"This is it, the dregs of glam rock. Weak and over-produced, if this band are our brightest hope for the future, then we are committing rock and roll suicide" – *Record Mirror*

**9 March** Corn Exchange, Cambridge
"Seven Seas of Rhye" reaches Number 10 in the UK charts.

**10 March** Greyhound, Croydon

**12 March** Roundhouse, Dagenham

**14 March** Town Hall, Cheltenham

**15 March** University, Glasgow

**16 March** University, Stirling
After a full show and three encores the audience is still not happy to let the band leave. A riot escalates and two people are stabbed. The next night's show is rescheduled until 2 April.

**19 March Winter** Gardens, Cleethorpes

**20 March** University, Manchester

**22 March** Civic Centre, Canvey Island, Essex

**23 March** Links Pavilion, Cromer, Norfolk

**24 March** Woods Leisure Centre, Colchester

**26 March** Palace Lido, Douglas, Isle of Man

**28 March** University of Aberystwyth

**29 March** The Gardens, Penzance

**30 March** Century Ballroom, Taunton

**31 March** Rainbow Theatre, London
"Seven Seas of Rhye" is added to the set.

**2 April** Barbarella's, Birmingham
The rescheduled show is now the last night of the tour. Roger bets the support act and crew that they will not streak across the stage. He loses the bet.

**3 April** Langham 1 Studio, London
Queen's final appearance at this venue. They record "Modern Times Rock 'N' Roll," "March of the Black Queen," "Nevermore" and "White Queen".

**9 April**
*Queen II* is released in the US to promote Queen's first American tour. It reaches Number 49. They are booked to play 19 shows with Mott the Hoople over four weeks.

**15 April**
The BBC session is broadcast.

**16 April** Regis College, Denver, Colorado
Queen's first gig in the US

**17 April** Memorial Hall, Kansas City, Missouri

**18 April** Keil Auditorium, St Louis, Missouri
Local reviews are not good: "Queen's onstage presence was an almost laughable bizarre mish-mash of every other more successful band of their genre".

**19 April** Fairgrounds Appliance Building, Oklahoma

**20 April** Mid South Coliseum, Memphis, Tennessee

**21 April** St Bernard Civic Center, New Orleans, Louisiana
Brian complains of pain but no problem can be diagnosed. The tour continues.

**26 April** Orpheum Theater, Boston, Massachusetts

**27 April** Palace Theater, Providence, Rhode Island

**28 April** Exposition Hall, Portland, Maine

**1 May** Farm Arena, Harrisburg, Pennsylvania
Queen argue with Aerosmith about running order but Brian befriends Joe Perry over a bottle of JD. "I played the whole show from memory," he recalls.

**2 May** Agricultural Hall, Allentown, Pennsylvania

**3 May** King's College, Wilkes Barre, Pennsylvania

**4 May** Palace Theater, Waterbury, Connecticut

**7-12 May** Uris Theater, New York
A five night "Mott the Hoople on Broadway" run. Brian collapses after the final show with suspected food poisoning. It turns out to be hepatitis. Kansas are drafted in to replace Queen on the tour and the band head home. Brian is worried he'll be replaced.

**June**
Roger and Freddie have solo shoots at Mick Rock's London studio (Freddie twice).

**June/July** Rockfield Studios, Gwent
Queen begin work on their third album. Brian contributes whenever he feels strong enough. Work moves briefly to Trident on 15 July.

**August**
Brian suffers a relapse and is diagnosed with a duodenal ulcer. September's North American tour is cancelled. Recording continues with gaps left for him to fill later. Brian writes "Now I'm Here" while in hospital and it is recorded from scratch when he returns to work. The rejuvenated Brian also has to play catch-up finishing off "Killer Queen," "She Makes Me" and "Brighton Rock." Apart from his own health, his great fear is that his bandmates will do without him: "'Killer Queen' is vintage Queen. The first time I heard Freddie playing that song, I was lying in my room in Rockfield feeling very sick and I remember hearing Freddie play this really great song and feeling sad,

because I thought, 'I can't even get out of bed to participate in this. Maybe the group will have to go on without me.' But then I got fixed up, thank God, and we were able to finish off 'Killer Queen.' They left some space for me and I did the solo. I had strong feelings about one of the harmony bits in the chorus, so we had another go at that too".

**August** Great Newport Street, London
Queen visit Mick Rock twice this month. Once for publicity shots for their overseas promotion and again to work on the album sleeve for their third album, *Sheer Heart Attack*. Unable to get the perfect shot, Mick cuts Roger's hair from one picture and adds it to another for the finished cover.

**September**
Elizabeth II lookalike Jeanette Charles presents the band with silver discs to commemorate 100,000 copies sold of *Queen II*.

**11 October**
EMI release Queen's third single, "Killer Queen" / "Flick of the Wrist," officially a double A-side although radios only play one song. Many charts list the single at Number 1, although it only reaches Number 2 in the BBC listings. After the drubbing of *Queen II*, it is nice to read good reviews: "Freddie Mercury comes through as a distinguished rock vocalist, and the backing, although complicated at times, is heard loud and clear" – *Sounds*; "Queen have come up with a sound that'll prove they aren't any one hit band" – *NME*.

**16 October** Maida Vale 4 Studio, London
Queen record their first BBC studio in its new home: "Now I'm Here," "Stone Cold Crazy," "Flick of the Wrist" and "Tenement Funster".

**21 October**
"Killer Queen" is released in America. It reaches Number 12.

**30 October** Palace Theatre, Manchester
The first night of Queen's Sheer Heat Attack tour: 19 concerts in 18 venues. Queen's recording of "God Save the Queen" is played to close the show for the first time.

**31 October** Victoria Hall, Hanley, Staffordshire

**1 November** Liverpool Empire
Fans rush the stage during the "Procession" tape and order has to be restored by the theatre manager. NME reviewer Tony Stewart is shocked by how good the show is. "Musically the band pull off an act that is both enjoyable and entertaining, shifting through apparent disparities in style that encompass white heat energy rock, vaudeville knees-up, melodic sophistication and high camp (witness the first part of their encore, 'Big Spender')".

**2 November** University, Leeds
Fans again rush the stage.

**3 November** Theatre, Coventry

**4 November**
The Maida Vale session is broadcast on the Bob Harris show. "Queen – one of the most exciting British bands to have emerged for a long time," says the host.

**5 November** City Hall, Sheffield

**6 November** St George's Hall, Bradford

**7 November** City Hall, Newcastle

**8 November** Apollo Theatre, Glasgow
Ten rows of seats are damaged when fans storm the stage and
Freddie is dragged into the throng.

EMI release Queen's third album, *Sheer Heart Attack* featuring
Mick Rock's "wasted" cover picture. It reaches Number 2
in the UK.

"Brighton Rock" (May)
"Killer Queen" (Mercury)
"Tenement Funster" (Taylor)
"Flick of the Wrist" (Mercury)
"Lily of the Valley" (Mercury)
"Now I'm Here" (May)
"In the Lap of the Gods" (Mercury)
"Stone Cold Crazy" (Deacon/May/Mercury/Taylor)
"Dear Friends" (May)
"Misfire" (Deacon)
"Bring Back that Leroy Brown" (Mercury)
"She Makes Me (Stormtrooper in Stilettos)" (May)
"In the Lap of the Gods... Revisited" (Mercury)

Still "no synths".

John's first recorded composition (never performed in concert).

Roger again sings his composition, "Tenement Funster." He also
writes the album's title song but it is not finished in time to
appear on the album, eventually released in 1977 on *News of
the World*.

"Stone Cold Crazy" is the reworked song from Freddie's
pre-Queen Wreckage days.

"Tenement Funster" runs through to "Lily of the Valley"
in one suite.

Metallica won a Grammy for their cover of "Stone Cold Crazy".

"Misfire" was covered by Neko Case in 1997.

Brian plays ukulele banjo on "Leroy Brown;" John plays
double bass.

John plays acoustic guitar on "She Makes Me".

### Reviews
"It ought to be pointed out to them that some of the best-loved groups in rock
history have contained members who didn't compose. Drummer Roger Taylor
and bassist John Deacon certainly don't do so with appreciable proficiency" –
*Phonographic Record*

"So each of Queen's four young pop princes has helped to prepare the band for
perhaps the heaviest, rockingest assault on these shores we've enjoyed in some
time. *Sheer Heart Attack* was the musical cement for their pact" – *Circus*

"*Sheer Heart Attack*, like its two predecessors, is a handsomely glossy
construction. If it's hard to love, it's hard not to admire: This band is skilled, after
all, and it dares" – *Rolling Stone*

"A feast. No duffers, and four songs that will just run and run: 'Killer Queen,' 'Flick
of the Wrist,' 'Now I'm Here' and 'In the Lap of the Gods...Revisited.' Even the
track I don't like, 'Brighton Rock,' includes May's Echoplex solo, still a vibrant,
thrilling experience whether you hear it live or on record" – *NME*

**9 November** University, Lancaster

**10 November** Guildhall, Preston

**12 November** Colston Hall, Bristol
*Sheer Heart Attack* is released in America. It reaches Number 12.

**13 November** Winter Gardens, Bournemouth

**14 November** Gaumont, Southampton

**15 November** Brangwyn Hall, Swansea

**16 November** Town Hall, Birmingham

**18 November** New Theatre, Oxford

**19/20 November** Rainbow Theatre, London
Both nights are filmed for possible release on screen or as
a live album.

**23 November** Konserthuset, Gothenburg, Sweden
The first of ten gigs in six countries on Queen's first "proper"
European tour. Their support is Lynyrd Skynyrd.

**25 November** Helsingin Kulttuuritalo, Helsinki, Finland

**27 November** Olympan, Lund

**28 November** Tivoli, Copenhagen

### December
Lawyer Jim Beach is brought in to negotiate Queen out of their
contract with Trident who still only pay them £60 per week.
Freddie has another solo shoot with Mick Rock, this time at
Freddie's home. It is the last official shoot although as a friend
Mick visits the band in the studio and onstage.

**1 December** 140 Theatre, Brussels

**2 December** Brienner Theatre, Munich

**4 December** Frankfurt

**5 December** Muskihalle, Hamburg

**6 December** Sporthalle, Cologne

**7 December** Siegen, Germany

**8 December** Congress Gebouw, The Hague, Netherlands

**10 December** Palacio de los Deportes, Barcelona
The final show of the tour. The 6,000 tickets sell out in
a day. *Record Mirror* runs a headline that claims: "Queen
conquer Europe".

### 1975
### 17 January
Queen's fourth single, and the second written by Brian,
is released. "Now I'm Here" is backed with "Lily of the Valley." It
reaches Number 11.

**18 January**
John Deacon marries Veronica Tetzlaff in London

**31 January** Beacon Theater, New York
Queen arrive to begin seven days of rehearsals ahead of their headlining 38-show tour. Support act is their earlier replacement, Kansas.

**5 February** Agora, Columbus, Ohio

**7 February** Palace Theater, Dayton Ohio

**8 February** Music Hall, Cleveland, Ohio
Two shows.

**9 February** Morris Civic Auditorium, Indiana

**10 February** Ford Auditorium, Detroit, Michigan

**11 February** Student Union, Toledo, Ohio

**14 February** Palace Theater, Waterbury, Connecticut

**15 February** Orpheum Theater, Boston
Two shows.

**16 February** Avery Fisher Hall, New York
Two shows. Freddie is interviewed afterwards by *Circus* magazine. "It was my idea entirely to do 'Big Spender.' I like that cabaretish sort of thing. I adore Liza Minnelli. Then I have to approach the others and convince them it's going to work"

**17 February** War Memorial, Trenton, New Jersey

**19 February** Armory, New York

**21 February** Capitol Theater, New Jersey

**22 February** Farm Arena, Harrisburg, Pennsylvania

**23 February** Erlinger Theater, Pennsylvania
Two shows. Freddie has voice problems and is told to rest for three months. He decides to attempt one more gig.

**24 February** Kennedy Center, Washington, Pennsylvania
Freddie gets a second opinion and gigs are only cancelled in Pittsburgh, Kuzton, Buffalo, Toronto, London and Davenport.

**5 March** Mary E Sawyer Auditorium, La Crosse, Wisconsin

**6 March** Madison, Wisconsin

**7 March** Uptown Theater, Milwaukee

**8 March** Aragon Ballroom, Chicago

**9 March** Keil Auditorium, St Louis

**10 March** Coliseum, Fort Wayne, Indiana

**12 March** Municipal Auditorium, Atlanta

**13 March** Civic Auditorium, Charleston, S Carolina

**15 March** Marina, Miami

**18 March** St Bernard Civic Auditorium, New Orleans

**20 March** Municipal Hall, San Antonio, Texas

**23 March** McFarlin Auditorium, Dallas

**25 March** Municipal Theater, Tulsa, Oklahoma

**29 March** Santa Monica Civic Auditorium, Los Angeles
Two shows.

**30 March** Winterland, San Francisco

**2 April** Kindmens, Alberta

**3 April** Calgary, Alberta

**6 April** Seattle, Washington
The band take a break in Hawaii before exploring their next unfamiliar territory.

**19 April** Budokan Hall, Tokyo
Queen's first trip to the Far East where they have become so popular. The overwhelming welcome is most unexpected. Queenmania has come to Japan. "I went into a shop to buy a tape recorder and the shop keeper said, "Ah so, you Queen" and proceeded to drag a camera from underneath the counter," recalls Roger. "He just kept taking pictures for about ten minutes. I couldn't get another word out of him".

**22 April** Aichi-ken Taiikukan, Nagoya

**23 April** Kokusai Taikan, Kobe

**25 April** Kyuden Taiikukan, Fukuoka

**28 April** Okayama-ken Taiikukan, Okayama

**29 April** Yamaha Tsumagoi Hall, Shizuoka

**30 April** Bunka Taiikukan, Yokohama

**1 May** Budokan Hall, Tokyo
The end of the Japanese tour.

**22 May**
Freddie is awarded an Ivor Novello in recognition of *"Killer Queen"*.

**August - November**
Queen begin work on their fourth album. In August they find time to help out fellow Trident artiste Eddie Howell on his track "Man From Manhattan." Mick Rock is on hand to capture the collaboration.

Jim Beach successfully extricates Queen from their three Trident contracts (the band pay the Sheffield brothers £100,000 for the privilege) and persuades Elton John's manager, John Reid, to take over the band's affairs.

**31 October**
Queen's fifth single is "Bohemian Rhapsody" / "I'm in Love with my Car." With promotion by stealth from DJ Kenny Everett it reaches Number 1 in the UK and stays there for nine weeks. In America the same combination hits Number 9. It is regarded as having the first "video" of the modern era. The film, shot at Elstree Studios by Bruce Gowers, opens with the band in their *Queen II* poses – just as Mick Rock had arranged them. It would later feature in *Wayne's World* and Queen's own "One Vision" video.

**14/15 November** Empire, Liverpool

The Night at the Opera tour kicks off at a familiar venue. New songs include the epic "Prophet's Song" and the harsher "Sweet Lady." Other fresh material will follow. The "opera bit" of "Bohemian Rhapsody" is not attempted live but it is incorporated in Kenny Everett's taped introduction, which opens the evening. Other songs include "Ogre Battle," "White Queen," "Flick of the Wrist," Medley: "Bohemian Rhapsody," "Killer Queen," "March of the Black Queen," "Bo Rhap" reprise, then "Bring Back that Leroy Brown," "Son and Daughter," "The Prophet's Song," "Stone Cold Crazy," "Doin' All Right," "Keep Yourself Alive," "Modern Times Rock 'N' Roll," "Seven Seas of Rhye," "Liar," "In the Lap of the Gods…Revisited" plus encores of "Now I'm Here," rock 'n' roll medley, "God Save the Queen".

**16 November** Coventry Theatre, Coventry

In a reminder of the Budokan shows, Freddie appears for the encore in a kimono

**17/18 November** Colston Hall, Bristol

**19 November** Capitol, Cardiff

**20 November**

Bruce Gower's "*Bohemian Rhapsody*" film is shown for the first time on *Top of the Pops*.

**21 November** Odeon, Taunton

EMI releases *A Night at the Opera*, Queen's most elaborate album yet. It sweeps to Number 1. The title is from a Marx Brothers film. The next year's LP, *A Day at the Races*, will continue the trend.

"Death on Two Legs (Dedicated to …)" (Mercury)
"Lazing on a Sunday Afternoon" (Mercury)
"I'm in Love with my Car" (Taylor)
"You're my Best Friend" (Deacon)
"39" (May)
"Sweet Lady" (May)
"Seaside Rendezvous" (Mercury)
"The Prophet's Song" (May)
"Love of my Life" (Mercury)
"Good Company" (May)
"Bohemian Rhapsody" (Mercury)
"God Save the Queen" (arr. Queen)

Still "no synths".

"Seaside Rendezvous" and "Good Company" are the only songs never performed onstage.

Taylor's song is dedicated to John Harris, longtime Queen tech.

The opening song is thought to be credited to one of the Trident team; on *Live Killers* Freddie's dedication is bleeped out.

*A Night at the Opera* is packaged in a gatefold sleeve with the Queen crest, designed by Freddie, on the front. The crest features a phoenix, then the symbols of each member's star sign.

Brian plays a toy Kyoto on "The Prophet Song" inspired by their Japanese tour.

John's "You're my Best Friend" becomes his first single. It reaches Number 7 in the UK and wins good reviews: "Beautiful harmonies, strident guitar chords and Freddie in superb voice," raved *Sounds*. "A fine record from one of the most diverse and exciting rock acts in years" added the *Sunday Freeman, NY*.

**Reviews**

"The overall impression is of musical range, power and consistently incisive lyrics. My hair is still standing on end – so if you like good music and don't mind looking silly, play this album" – *Melody Maker*

"Queen appears ready to make its mark in North America. The group's potential is practically limitless, indicating that Queen is destined to finally take its place among the small handful of truly major acts working in rock today" – *Winnipeg Free Press*

**23 November** Winter Gardens, Bournemouth

**24 November** Gaumont, Southampton

**25 November**

While still in Southampton, the band discover "Bohemian Rhapsody" is Number 1 in the UK.

**26 November** Free Trade Hall, Manchester

Two shows.

**29/30 November** Hammersmith Odeon, London

"Brighton Rock" is reintroduced to the set incorporating the "guitar solo" that began in Smile's "Blag" and transferred to "Son and Daughter".

**1/2 December** Hammersmith Odeon, London

"It's certainly already a great show and, by the time they've had a chance to include one or more extra numbers from the new album (there are only three in the set at the moment) it should be even better" – *Record Mirror*

**7 December** Civic Hall, Wolverhampton

**8 December** Guildhall, Preston

**9/10 December** Odeon, Birmingham

**11 December** City Hall, Newcastle

After the show plain clothed police officers search the band for drugs.

**13 December** Caird Hall, Dundee

**14 December** Capitol, Aberdeen

**15/16 December** Apollo Theatre, Glasgow

**24 December** Hammersmith Odeon, London

"Queen are well on their way to becoming one of Britain's biggest bands and Kenny Everett is playing them to death – what more could you want? Britain's most regal band awaits your presence" – *Melody Maker*. The Christmas Eve show is broadcast live on both Radio One and *The Old Grey Whistle Test*. The show is a firm fans' favorite but Brian recalls it being a struggle for the band: "Freddie and I had dreadful flu and could hardly walk, let alone play, so it wasn't one of our greatest performances." Brian's and Freddie's parents meet for the first time

**1976**

On the crest of a wave, Queen begin the year at Number 1 in both the album and singles charts. It is the beginning of their lives as superstars. Sixteen years later the same song would top the charts again. This time it is the end of an era.

# ACKNOWLEDGMENTS

Mick Rock wishes to thank the following for making this book happen:

Freddie, Brian, Roger and John for being such great subjects;
Colin Webb for taking care of business in his inimitable way;
Adrian Cross for his terrific design eye;
Jeff Hudson for his insightful foreword;
Victoria Webb for staying on top of everyone and making all the elements come together.

Mick also wishes to express his gratitude to the following:

Pati Rock, Nathalie Rock, Brian Roylance, Andrew Oldham, Allen Klein, Iris Keitel, Cathy Roylance, Joan Rock, Richard Lasdon, Liz Vap, Catherine Alexander, Dean Holtermann, Sat Jivan Kaur, Sat Jivan Singh, Nick Roylance, Robert Urband, Lucky and Shazi of Station Labs, NYC, Andrew Melchior

This book is dedicated to the memory of the amazing Freddie Mercury and his extraordinary talents.

*"There are no accidents. Anything that comes to you, you have put out beams for it."* Yogi Bhajan

*"For the great artist death is never the end. It is the beginning of his affair with eternal beauty."* Gerard De Nerval

**www.mickrock.com**

MICK ROCK 2007. Photograph © copyright Pati Rock
Opposite page MICK ROCK RIPART